TEXAS WOMAN WIDOWED TWICE AND BECOMING AN EAGLE

Danva York Meister

WESTBOW
PRESS
A DIVISION OF THOMAS NELSON

ISBN: 978-1-4497-4844-9 (sc)
ISBN: 978-1-4497-4845-6 (hc)
ISBN: 978-1-4497-4843-2 (e)

WestBow Press books may be ordered through booksellers or by contacting:

WestBow Press
A Division of Thomas Nelson
1663 Liberty Drive
Bloomington, IN 47403
www.westbowpress.com
1-(866) 928-1240

Library of Congress Control Number: 2012908784

Printed in the United States of America

WestBow Press rev. date: 06/04/2012

CONTENTS

FOREWORD

THE GRIEF THAT COMES FROM LOSING a loved one oftentimes can be more than we can bear. But the grief from losing not one but two husbands could easily seem insurmountable. That is exactly what Danva York Meister experienced. In this book, *Texas Woman Widowed Twice and Becoming an Eagle,* Danva reveals the pain, loneliness, and agony that come from being twice widowed, as well as the amazing grace, joy, and freedom she discovered along the way.

God has given Danva incredible insight and revelation when it comes to dealing with fear, grief, loneliness, and despair. Although the walls in her life were broken down, her desperate cry for help from the Lord allowed her to succeed in repairing them. As a result of doing so, not only has her strength been renewed, but now the Lord has given her that same grace to help strengthen the lives of others.

From fear to freedom, from loneliness to loving, from isolation to celebration, Danva has learned how to rejoice again! God alone has turned her mourning into dancing! Through many tears, she now can reveal the secret of triumphing over the enemy during the darkness hours of the soul. No matter the pain or the suffering, she has learned how to praise the Lord through it all. God has placed a new melody in her heart. He is the song that she now joyfully sings.

Danva along with her wonderful husband Howard are faithful members of the church that I pastor in Bedford, Texas. God has placed them as shining lights within our congregation. What an honor and a privilege it was for me to perform the wedding ceremony for this precious couple. As I have gotten to know them better, I can tell you firsthand that their ministry to the body of Christ will help to restore hope, joy, and strength to those who are walking under the cloud of loneliness, brokenness, and grief.

The revelations in this book came at a great price to Danva. As you read it, you will discover incredible insights and wisdom on how to forget the pain of the past and press on toward the glorious future that awaits you.

It is my sincere prayer that *Texas Woman Widowed Twice and Becoming an Eagle* finds its way into the hands of many who are hurting and dealing with grief. Danva's incredible and inspiring story will encourage your heart and help you to believe again.

With this book, you will learn how to run and not be weary, to walk and not faint, to be strengthened and renewed as you soar on wings like eagles!

Floyd L. Ellsworth

Senior pastor, Oasis Community Worship Center

*Pastors Floyd and Michelle Ellsworth and they are dear to my heart.
They encouraged me to write my book. Pastor Floyd found Westbow
Press for me and I am blessed to have them as my pastors.*

To my precious children Doug and Angela MacLeod, Jim and Claudanna Sanner, Claude and Melanie York, Sammy York, and Anju Chettri.

And precious grandchildren Bethany Mitchell, Caleb MacLeod, Austin MacLeod, Jeremy and Lauren Francis, Andrea Sanner, Tessa York, and Aylisa Anthony.

You all mean so much to me. I thank you for your love and for helping me with pictures or whatever I needed for my book. The comforting everyone gave me through the promotion of Claude, your dad and papa, has inspired me. I have seen your own hurt, and I pray this book can help you. We are helping each other. Soon Jesus will come and take us to heaven, and we will see Claude again. He is not dead. He is just away in heaven and he is in our future.

May God's love like waves of peace come and rest upon all of you.

Love, Mom and Nana

Our family picture was taken by Austin, last Christmas 2011

Dorian Ray, Jeremy and Lauren's son and our first great grandson.

To my precious daughter Angela.

I know you do not remember your first dad, because you were too young. He loved you very much and was so proud of you. I know, through the years, you wished you could have known him and did not understand why God took him to heaven. But you were blessed to have two dads to love you.

I felt a double responsibility to be both mom and dad to you, because he was not with us anymore. That is why I was so overly protective of you. Eddie is looking down from heaven and sees how great his little girl turned out. You will get to meet him in heaven someday. Then you can talk to him and get to know him.

May God grant to you and Eddie as much time in heaven as you need to get to know each other.

I love you,

Mom

Danva, Angela with Eddie and I wish we
could have had more time together.

Acknowledgments

To Patty Perry my precious friend and neighbor.

 Thank you so very much for proofreading my book and for using your gifts and talents to put a special touch to my book as you took the time to read through it. I saw sparkles of joy as you made comments and took the time to point them out to me. You encouraged me and desired excellence in helping me present a book that would be a help to others. You are a blessing to me!

 Friends are friends forever.

 I love you,

 Danva

To Cindy Nordyke.

 Thank you for encouraging me to write a book about what I was going through. You said, "A book can take you where you cannot go." Thank you for your godly life through the years I have known you. You have been an inspiration to me and many other people. Also, thank you for all the information you gave to help me on my journey.

 Friends are friends forever. I love you Danva

To Lena Dooley.

 Thank you for teaching me your ideas on book writing. You came highly recommended, and I have seen the books you have written. I feel honored for you to be helping me. I know the knowledge that I have received from you will broaden my ability to write books in the future. You shared with me that God put inside of us, even when we were in our mothers' wombs, the ability to write books. I do desire that and to have the quality of being wise. I do give God all the glory for anything He blesses my hands to do.

 My book-writer friend, I love you.

 Danva

To Pamela Guerrieri and Kimberly Jace, my editors.

Thank you for the evaluation of my book. This constitutes completeness of my desire for my book. You have wisdom and excellence in your work. Your name for your company Proofed to Perfection fits you perfectly. God anointed you and set you apart for such a time as this, to edit my book with apparent loyalty and precise service. Your understanding me and encouraging me was a blessing. My hurt turned into my book for others. I wanted them to see there was light at the end of the tunnel in my life, and you saw this too. Your confidence in me and my book has made me see the significance of my writing. Your kind words and how my story blessed you brought tears to my eyes. I realized it is for such a time as this that my book had to be written. I am giving God all the glory.

I thank God for you,

Love,

Danva

To Rory Day, Mary Endicott, Dustin Pike, Zackery Wood, Bill Whitfill, Daniel Digiavanni, Heather Piper, Julia Bright, Katie Echels and Kathryn Applin.

Thank you all for your devoted help and time you spent with my project. You took your time to teach me things on my computer to enhance my knowledge. I am grateful to God for all of you. You blessed the widow and there is blessing coming to all of you for your kindness. Zack you were there for me in the finishing touches and I could not have done without you or any of the staff. You have all become my friends at Office Depot.

My friends we are friends forever.

Love

Danva

To Mama Miller, Dorothy Curington, Claude York Sr., Bethany Mitchell, Austin MacLeod, Jim Sanner, Charlotte Yeathermon, Kenny and Nancy Southard, Wanda Woods, Wendy Bennie, George and Wanda Salazar, Laura Gross, Gloria Torres, Julia Bright, Lexi Van Bunnen, Jerry Brown, Peri Hughes owner of Barron's, Mark Jean, Karen Meister, Kathy Meister, Carla Hamilton, Ciara Johnson and Jessica Azzinnari.

Thank you all for all the pictures you helped me with for my book. My book can now have wonderful memories for all to see. You took the time to stop lend you work and bless my life and my book. Your work will live in my book and all can look and say well done.

From my heart I can say I love all of you.

Love,

Danva

To Jeremy Weddle, Richard Robertson, Dustin Gearlds, Becky Dulin, Heather Pund, Sam Fitzgerald, Brie Mengel, Megan Leiter, Todd Greer, Rebecca Dille, Ryan Briggs all the Westbow Press Team of Thomas Nelson.

It is a great honor to be accepted by your company. Thank you for accepting my book and publishing it for me. All the people I have worked with on my book have been a great help to me. There are many details that are involved in producing a book. I am grateful for all who have been patient with me as I stepped into a new learning process. All the different departments I have dealt with have been an asset for me and are wonderful people to work with. I was impressed and had peace from all the conversations I had with the team. I can say, "I am well pleased." I know you were chosen by God to publish my book.

God bless all of you.

Love,

Danva

Introduction

I WANT TO SHARE MY STORY OF my two marriages and the promotion of two wonderful men. I was married to Clyde Edward Williams for three years. He went by the name Eddie. My marriage to Claude Ray York, Sr. lasted forty-four years.

Since I've been widowed twice, I want to be an eagle for God and learn to stand alone with Jesus. I have to remember that birds fly in flocks and eagles fly alone. I know I couldn't do this without Jesus helping me, but I can do all things through Jesus who infuses inner strength into me, as the Bible says in Philippians 4:13 (AMP).

I've had to step into my unknown future and trust God to lead me. I will receive God's plan for me by faith, as in James 1:5–8 (AMP) and I know it will not come out of the natural but the supernatural power of God. The Lord will bless me with peace, as in Psalm 29:11.

This is one way I know I am in the will of God: I have peace no matter what is happening around me. God is helping me to take my rightful place in this earth. God is teaching me how to walk and stand. I've asked God to create in me a clean heart so that my eyes can become the windows of my soul. I want God to increase in my life, and I must decrease as in the book of John 3:30.

I have made this confession to my God: God, you are my keeper, and I am not my keeper, as it says in Psalm 121:5 and 8. I trust you, God, to keep me. God, I will not be afraid to commit my unknown future to you, my known God. All I have to do is believe. When I face the impossible, a miracle is possible.

God looked at me in the spirit realm and saw the plan He had for me while I was in my mother's womb, as in Psalm 139:13–16. I became righteous the day I became saved, so God sees my spirit as perfect. Being widowed twice, I've come to the conclusion that I still have something to do for God, something I have not yet fulfilled. I want to discover the plan God has for me.

When I have completed my purpose in life, I will rise when God calls my name. I will rise on eagle's wings, because Jesus will have helped me become an eagle. I will have won the victory.

I pray my book can be an encouragement to others to fight the good fight of faith and hold onto Jesus, who is the source of our comfort, as in 2 Corinthians 1:3–4.

I have anointed myself with oil, I have claimed Psalm 45:1, and I have prayed for God to help me write this book. I confess that my heart does overflow with a goodly theme, and my tongue is like the pen of a ready writer.

Chapter One

LIFE WITH EDDIE

1961

I MET EDDIE WILLIAMS AT MY SIXTEENTH birthday party, which my friend Elsie Cummings threw for me at her house. I didn't know she had invited Eddie, but that night ended up being the first day of the rest of my life.

As I primped for the party, my mother baked a big birthday cake for me. We had so much fun that night at the party, and Eddie and I hit it off from the beginning. Soon after, Eddie asked me for a date, and love embraced us.

One day, Eddie came to see me at my school, Rio Vista High School in Rio Vista, Texas, and he asked me to go to his car with him. I wondered why he had shown up out of the blue and why he wanted me to follow him to the car. As my curiosity mounted, I began to grab that moment, and I got excited about it. I thought it must be important for him to drive all the way from Fort Worth to see me in the middle of the day—especially when I was still in school.

Being a Texas girl, with big Texas thoughts, I rolled ideas around in my head. Were we going to the Texas State Fair? Or he could have been taking me horseback riding, which I loved to do. Or maybe he was going to buy me a horse!

All kinds of thoughts raced through my mind. I began to imagine some lavish, important event, although I couldn't figure out what it would be.

When we got into his car, I started talking. "What is so important that it would make you come to my school to see me?"

He avoided my question and changed the subject, just talking about anything and everything, being nonchalant.

Then, all of a sudden, he asked, "Will you marry me?"

I could not even imagine that this was why Eddie had come to see me that day! I pondered and paused, and then a smile crept across my lips. "I have only one thing to say to you, and that is yes!" I exclaimed.

He gave me a small box, and I opened it up; inside was an engagement ring. "It is so beautiful!" I said. I was so happy.

A month later, Eddie wanted to have a serious talk. "I have been drafted into the army," he said, "so we will have to put off the wedding."

I was disappointed, but I knew there was nothing we could do. Apparently, God had something else in mind. But first, Eddie had to get a physical, and he didn't pass it. So the wedding was back on.

Eddie and I were married at Crestmont Baptist Church in Burleson, Texas. We had a very nice wedding. I sang "I Love You Truly" to Eddie during the ceremony.

Eddie, Danva with wedding group.

Eddie, Danva with parents Robert, Quilla, Oscar, Dorothy.

Eddie, Danva just married and walking down the aisle.

Eddie, Danva with our wedding cake my Aunt Geraldine bought for us.

Daia, Quilla, Berniece, Eddie's Mother, sisters that I love dearly.

After the wedding was over, we had to climb through a window to leave because Eddie's friends were trying to play a trick on us to separate us for the night. Someone had warned us about their plot, so we escaped. Eddie's friends were all good people, but they liked to play around.

I was a young bride of seventeen. Nine months later, I gave birth to my first child, Angela.

Eddie and I both adored our daughter. Eddie had to go out of town on his job. Angela had just been born, and I did not want to be alone. I went to stay with my parents, Oscar and Dorothy Curington. This was better for me since my mother could help me get used to motherhood. Mother made Angela a bed out of a dresser drawer. My daddy would help me during the night when she woke up. In the middle of the night, Angela would be wide-awake, looking at us happily. But if we turned the light off, she would start crying. Daddy would warm her bottle and help me feed her.

Then Eddie and I moved close to Eddie's parents, Robert and Quilla Williams, where we lived for three months. They loved Angela very much and often took her places with them. I was close to Eddie's family. We all liked having fun together. Quilla would buy Eddie, Angela, and me matching Western shirts. Angela was so cute in her tiny Western wear. We all were born in Texas, so we liked that Western style.

One day, when Eddie's sisters, Berniece and Daia, came home from church, Eddie and their other brother, Shorty, started making fun of Daia.

"Leave her alone!" I told them. "She is so cute, and she is sincere about God, so don't bother her anymore. It wouldn't hurt any of you to go to church too."

Daia, Berniece and I became good buddies. We all stood up for each other, and we walked a lot together around the north side of Fort Worth.

Eddie and I liked to ride horses, and we did this a lot. We also liked to dance. Many people in our neighborhood would go to the Wagon Wheel, which had a big band. Harlan and Alice York owned the Wagon Wheel. We were like a big family when we all got together.

Eddie, Angela, and I were in a horrible car wreck.

Eddie wearing his Texas cowboy hat and Danva is holding Angela.

We had gone to Oklahoma to bring my sister, Barbara Ann, to Texas. Two days later, we took her back to Oklahoma. We were on our way home when the accident happened. Eddie and I were both tired. I had just taken Angela out of her infant seat and was holding her; Eddie was at the wheel. We both just fell asleep. Then I heard Eddie shout, "Danva, we are going to flip over!" Fear gripped me! I knew there was nothing that I could do except to hold on to Angela as tightly as I could. As we flipped,

I felt my head hit the top of the pickup. My life passed before me in that instant.

I didn't know if this was going to be the last day of our lives. I felt such anguish and pain as the pickup rolled over and over, ten times, until it knocked me out. I was a Christian, but I did not know how to take my authority then, as I know now.

It must not have been our time to go to heaven because we survived, even though the pickup was flattened. Angels must have come to our rescue. I remember waking up in the ambulance and asking, "Where is my baby?"

The emergency workers told me she was fine, but I screamed, "I can't hear her!" I looked up at one of the workers in desperation. "Spank her and make her cry so I can hear her voice," I pleaded.

He didn't really want to, but, after I insisted, he gave poor Angela a little smack. She started crying. When I heard her, I was so relieved.

Then I remembered my husband and called to him. "Eddie? Where's Eddie?" I was frantic.

"He's right here in the ambulance, lying on a stretcher just like you are," the man explained.

"Eddie, are you all right?" I shouted. I couldn't keep the panic out of my voice.

I could hear him wince as he replied, "I'm in a lot of pain, Danva. I think the pickup landed on my back."

I ached for him, but there was nothing else I could do.

After we arrived at the hospital, doctors put Angela in an oxygen tent. "Why are you doing that?" I asked. I wanted so badly to hold my baby, not look at her through a tent.

"Do you know what happened out there?" a nurse asked.

"We were in a wreck."

"Yes, and after the truck tumbled around, your baby was just lying on the highway," the nurse said. "A lady stopped and picked her up to keep any cars from hitting her."

Tears streamed down my face. I praise God that a stranger saw Angela and was quick to pick her up. My baby only had a little cut on her head. I knew she could have been killed, and it was very heart wrenching for me, especially being her mom, to hear this. I think taking Angela out of the plastic infant seat might have actually saved her from being crushed in the truck.

But I felt that I had not held onto Angela tightly enough. I had failed to protect her. All through her life, I was an overprotective mother. I was that way with my other two children, Claudanna and Claude Jr., too. They probably did not understand, but it all went back to me thinking that I did not hold on tightly enough to Angela during that accident.

I understand now that it was out of my control because I was knocked unconscious. But I made a decision: "No matter what, I am going to be a good mother. I'll protect Angela and all my children the best that I can."

In those days, there were no infant car safety seats or even safety belts. I think that in our situation, that was a blessing. We would have all died if we had been strapped into the truck, because it ended up smashed and flattened. If we had not been thrown from the pickup, we would not have survived. Of course, we all had an angel watching over us, and someone was praying for us.

Eddie's back was so badly injured that doctors put him in a special bed. I had a broken arm, a broken finger, and cuts up and down my legs. When I got to the hospital, they looked at my legs and immediately cut off my slacks to assess the damage. I still have a scar from one of those deep gashes in my leg.

Praise God, we did survive. It was a miracle. When we finally were well enough to go home, I had to learn to feed Angela with my left hand, because my right arm and finger were both in a cast.

Eddie's job took him to Graham, Texas, to work. I went with him, and we rented a house. One night, we went to a church there and Eddie walked to the altar. He asked Jesus into his heart. I was so proud of him. God knew what would unfold in the future.

Tragedy struck our home not long after that accident. Eddie was on the job at Lufkin, Texas. He had climbed a forty-five-foot utility pole, which is the equivalent of four and a half stories high, without a safety belt, to work on the crossbar of the pole. When he raised his head, it came in contact with the electrical current, and he fell.

In reality, he was not even supposed to be climbing the pole. He was only supposed to hand tools to the linemen who were trained to do this. According to the *Fort Worth Press* article, this occurred around 3:00 p.m. He was taken to a local hospital.

I was working at Texas Instruments in Dallas when I got a call from the police who said my husband had been burned and hurt very badly. I waited for Eddie's parents, Robert and Quilla, his brother, Shorty, and his sisters, Berniece and Daia, to pick me up. They stopped to eat on the way to Lufkin, but I couldn't eat anything. I just wanted to get to the hospital.

It seemed like an eternity before we arrived at the hospital. When we arrived, a doctor came out and told us that Eddie had died. Quilla and I screamed and cried. I rushed outside the hospital, and I started to run.

I talked to myself as I ran, and I was running very fast. "I do not want to believe this," I told myself. "I have to run away from what they just told me. This is not true. I have to run faster and faster, because then this will go away. I will wake up, and it will be only a dream."

The next thing I knew, Eddie's brother Shorty grabbed me. I said, "Let me go! Let me go!" But he would not let go of me, and he took me back to the hospital. They gave Quilla and me shots to knock us out.

I woke up in a motel room remembering the painful loss of my husband and hearing people talking about it. I was scared to face the death of my husband at such a young age. Now I had a baby to bring up in the world by myself.

I had accepted Jesus as my Savior when I was nine years old, and I read my Bible and always prayed, but I did not know how to deal with death. I had no wisdom about how to handle money issues or make any decisions regarding finances.

Because Eddie was killed on the job, I was given a lump sum of money. I began a savings account for Angela with her settlement. With my money, I paid the funeral expenses and bought a car. I remember thinking, *be sure you have a good car to drive, because you will be alone most of the time now.* Buying a car made me feel more secure. I knew that I would have transportation when I needed it.

I spent the rest of the money here and there. I did not invest any of it. Before I noticed, the money was gone. I would suggest to anyone that, whatever money he or she receives, he or she should pray for wisdom in budgeting. Invest what money you can spare so you can earn money on your investment.

I had to make decisions at the Lufkin Funeral Home, and I needed my parents to be there with me. They were driving down and arrived later. At twenty, I was still so young, and I had to make adult decisions that I had never made before. I had two funeral home bills: one from the funeral home in Lufkin, and another from a funeral home in Fort Worth, where we transferred Eddie's body.

The Williams family had a cemetery plot for him at Poolville, Texas, so I did not have to pay for that.

I had to decide what clothes to dress him in. He almost never wore a suit, although he had worn one at our wedding. I decided go to a Western clothing store and pick out some clothes for Eddie to be buried in. Eddie loved his Western outfits. His parents agreed with my decision.

My advice to women or men is to take out a burial policy while you are young, because it will cost you less than when you become older. Knowing that you have taken care of this helps relieve the stress that comes later. If Eddie had not been killed on his job, I would have had no way of paying all those hospital and funeral expenses.

I cried so much that I just started wearing sunglasses all the time. I felt it kept people from seeing my hurt. I did not want them to even recognize me and ask me questions. I just needed my space to grieve in my own way.

When we got back to our apartment in Fort Worth, I found a note from Eddie saying that he loved me and he had taken Angela to Mrs. Park's house because he was going to Lufkin to work. It was such a hard thing to know I would not see Eddie there anymore. Memories of our love and our life surrounded me there. I felt I had to get another apartment after the funeral.

The funeral was so very hard to go through. I remember just being in a daze. As we were leaving the grave, I wanted them to open the casket so Angela and I could say good-bye to Eddie one more time. My daddy thought it would be too hard for me. He wanted to protect me, so he put me in the car and would not let me out.

I screamed, "Let me out! I want us to say one more good-bye!"

Finally, he agreed to let me say one more good-bye. They opened the casket, and Angela and I kissed Eddie and said our last good-byes. This was the closure I needed.

I would say to anyone whose loved one has suffered a great loss, "Let the one who is grieving do what he or she wants to." Believe me, the people have set in their hearts what they need to do, and it does bring them closure.

When my daddy passed, my mother wanted to get in the bed with him. Some said for her not to, but I said they should let her, because that was her closure. She put her arms around my daddy and just cried and loved on him.

I think death is the hardest thing on earth to go through. Missing those who die and knowing they will not be here to talk to anymore leaves you with such an empty feeling. Now that my second husband has passed away, I feel that again. That is when we have to trust in Jesus to help us!

On May 19, 1965, my uncle, Bobby Miller, wrote me a touching letter. I will never forget his kind words of encouragement. He said, "Danva, the Lord works in ways sometimes that make it difficult for people to understand why things happen the way they do. But if one stops and realizes that we are richly blessed already, we will continue to be blessed and that will give some comfort. I know you loved Eddie and will miss him. Now more than anything else, you have your baby, Angela, to love and care for. It will require a great deal of willpower, devotion, and love to get over the first big hurdles. Knowing you as well as I do, Danva, and knowing that you will always let God lead you, in this time of sorrow and in years to come you will make out fine." How his words still minister to me even forty-five years later.

Life is too short. I want to encourage you to spend quality time with whomever you love. Tell them how much you love them. Just call them on the phone and talk with them and let them know you love them. Some people might say, "Oh, they know I love them!" But you have to tell them, because we all need to hear that.

When you let people know you love them, you bring out the best in you by showing them that you care. You may not be able to do it tomorrow—so do it today.

Eddie lives on through his daughter and grandchildren. Everyone in the family has noticed, while looking at family photos, that Austin—Angela's second son—looks like Eddie. Even Austin said he noticed that. He said he was proud to look like him.

Chapter Two

LIFE WITH CLAUDE

ANGELA AND I HAD MOVED TO a duplex, and we had a nice neighbor who lived in a house nearby. She started babysitting for Angela while I was at work.

I still worked at Texas Instruments in Dallas. It was a long drive to Dallas, but I had a very good job. My life was quite different after Eddie's death, but I felt I had to go on because I had a daughter to take care of.

My high school friend, Lyda, and her husband, Bob, came from Ohio to see me. Bob advised me to open a business with the money I had received in the settlement from Eddie's death, but I told him I knew nothing about operating a business. I wish he had taught me what I needed to know. Eventually, I spent the money.

At the time, there was no one else advising me to invest my money. I have learned a lot since then. I am glad that I understand now to invest and save money.

My parents had taught me to tithe as a young girl, and I am so grateful to them for that. I paid my tithe out of whatever I received or earned, and I always paid it based on the gross amount.

God has taken care of me. He began to show me how to budget my money. I have helped others learn how to budget, something I learned later, during my marriage to Claude. I have included the budget template I use at the end of this book.

Growing up and learning how to do things the right way is part of life. I thank God for His grace and teaching me along the path of my life. One *night*, a married man who lived in the duplex next to me came to my door. He was drunk. That event really scared me, so I called a nice man I knew from the Wagon Wheel. His name was Claude York. He was the nephew of Harlan, the Wagon Wheel's owner.

I told Claude I was scared, and he came right over and told the man not to come to my door anymore. Claude seemed like a hero to me. After that, Claude started coming over to check on me. I was lonely and I appreciated his concern. We started dating.

One day, one of Eddie's friends called and said he wanted to talk to me. He asked if I would go somewhere with him. I decided to go, because I thought I would be safe.

He drove us to a secluded place and stopped his car. "I heard you are dating Claude," he began. "I want you to know that I do not want you to date Claude."

I replied, "That is not any of your business. I may be twenty years old, but I have a mind of my own! I don't need you bossing me around."

"The reason is because I want to marry you," he said.

I was angry. "I do not want to marry you," I said. "I am not your girlfriend, and you have no right to demand such a thing of me."

When he leaned closer to me, I screamed. "Don't you dare touch me, and I mean it!"

Then he pulled out a gun and put it to my head.

My life passed before me again, just as it had when Eddie and I were in that wreck. When you face death, it is a horrible nightmare. The sting of death was still hovering over me because of Eddie's death. I had not dealt with it and did not know how to.

"If you don't marry me," he said, "I'll kill you."

Fear gripped me. But then, suddenly, peace came over me. I told him, "In view of the fact that I do not want to marry you, you will just have to kill me." Even with the gun still being pointed toward my head, I felt an irrepressible joy that came from my consciousness of God's favor and protection.

He looked stunned, but I was not afraid because I knew God was with me.

I knew that God was preserving my life because I was His child and He was delivering me from the hand of the wicked. I was so grateful to God that I said, "I thank you, God, for sparing my life."

The angels of the Lord were protecting me, and I could sense them all around me. The man put away the gun and drove me back home and let me out of the car. He never bothered me again. I do believe that my angel was with me that day, because Eddie's friend had a loaded gun and I believe he meant to use it.

When I told Claude what had happened, he took me in his arms. "I want to marry you and protect you," he said. "I want to help you raise Angela and become her daddy."

I looked at Claude and felt so touched and delighted. "Let me kiss you," I said. "This kiss is to embrace you with gratefulness for who you are and for wanting to take care of us. I want to be your wife. I will be happy to marry you, because I trust you with my life and happiness."

"The happiness will not just be for me but for Angela too," I continued as tears welled up in my eyes. "I know she needs a daddy, and you two already have a relationship and enjoy each other. My answer to you is yes! I know God has brought us together too."

What a prize of a man he became to Angela and me! I call him "God-sent and appointed" to take us in his arms to shelter us, the same way Jesus would.

Claude had been married before and the marriage did not work out. Claude had a son named Sammy from this marriage. Claude would get him on weekends, and he was a good daddy. Sammy was excited to have a future new sister.

I felt a release of fear. My worries about being alone in my future instantly left me. I went into an ecstasy of joy and excitement to know someone else would love me again and I would feel happiness again.

I can describe this part of my journey as an unfolding; it took the next forty-four years. Claude's love was like a refreshing, wet, face cloth that gave me a wake-up jolt. He awakened me to my happiness and reminded me of the importance of what God had brought into my life: this wonderful man, Claude.

We began to make plans for our wedding. One month later, we traveled to Durant, Oklahoma, so we could have privacy. My best friend, Judy Bolinger, went with us. We stopped at the courthouse to get our marriage license. We asked the clerk if he knew of a minister who would marry us, and he sent us to a minister's home.

We had our wedding there at the minister's home. It was a small, nice ceremony. I wore a blue chiffon dress. I still have my wedding dress, forty-four years later. Claude wore a black suit, and he looked so handsome.

Claude and Danva wedding picture and we included Angela.

My world was changing fast. I was happy again.

Claude told me that, before he met me, he would go to church and wait on the steps until it opened. He said he had always gone to church with his parents and he still loved going to church. Claude had a tender heart for God and Jesus, his Lord.

After we returned to Texas, we decided to buy a house in Burleson. I was glad to move from the north side of Fort Worth.

We had our first Christmas in Burleson. Claude stayed up all night putting together a swing set for Angela in our cold garage. I could see I had made a good choice by marrying Claude. He loved me and also loved Angela. He treated her like his own daughter.

Through the years, my experience shows that spirit is stronger than blood. You would never know that Claude and Angela were not biological dad and daughter. I do thank God that we both felt so secure with Claude. He is our hero.

Two months after we were married, I became pregnant with our daughter, Claudanna. When she was born, her daddy could not keep his eyes off her. He stayed at the nursery window while looking at her more than he stayed in the room with me.

I was so glad he was happy and proud. Claude wanted to name our new baby after himself and his Mother Zoetta, so we did. Claudanna Zoe York is her full name. When we brought Claudanna home from the hospital, Angela loved her too. They became so close to each other. Angela was three years old. At such a young age, she looked at Claudanna with such love and said, "Mommy, is she my baby and can I play with my baby doll?" She wanted to stay close to her and hold her. I replied, "You go sit on the couch and you can hold her with someone's assistance. She is our new baby and specially yours too. We just have to be careful with her because she is a real baby."

Sammy had been excited about having Angela for a sister, and now he was just as excited to have Claudanna for a sister too. He said, "She is tiny and very pretty, and I want to hold her too." I let him hold her, and he cuddled her up to his face and kissed her. Their first meeting was a sweet scene.

Claude and Zoetta (Claude's parents) kept Angela while I was in the hospital. Claude's parents loved their children and grandchildren.

Claude parents Claude, Zoetta, Joe his brother,
Wanda his sister and Claude.

One day, Claude came home with a tiny kitten in one of his pockets and a tiny puppy in his other. He put Angela and Claudanna in Claudanna's baby bed and then set the kitten and the puppy in the baby bed too, and then he took a picture. They became a part of our family and grew up with our children.

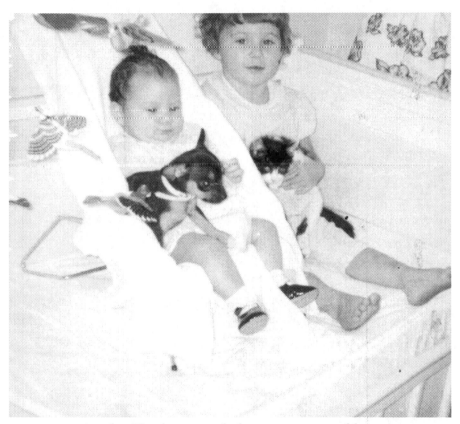

Angela, Claudanna, with their new puppy and kitty.

I keep that photo in an album and I just thought of it the other day when I was shopping. I went to a store where Claude liked to shop. I never liked that shop as much as he did, but it makes me feel close to him to go to places he enjoyed. I saw a large, framed picture that reminded me of Claude: a little girl holding a little kitten in one hand and a puppy in the other. I instantly loved this picture. I did end up buying it and hung it up in my home.

Missing Claude has been very hard for me. We were married forty-four years, so I have many memories. So this is how I have learned to be comforted. Sometimes, I go where Claude liked to go. I even enjoy talking to him as I shop.

At my kitchen window every morning, I look to the sky and ask Claude, "What are you doing in heaven today, honey? I know you are having the best time you have ever had, and I am so happy for you, but I do miss you, my sweetheart."

I know he is in heaven. He is not dead but alive with Jesus! He is not in his physical body but in his spiritual body. As I walk by the picture that I bought, it always reminds me of Claude. I smile knowing how he made our daughters so happy with the kitten and the puppy.

Our favorite place to go was Galveston, Texas. I became pregnant with our son, Claude Jr., one summer when we vacationed there.

When I was pregnant with Claude Jr., I craved strawberry shortcake. I would tell Claude, "I have to have some strawberry shortcake, and I have to have it right now! Will you please go get me some?"

"Yes, I will," Claude would say, and he'd set off at any hour to buy it for me.

Claude Jr. was born three years after Claudanna, and they were always close to each other. Of course, Claude Sr. was proud of him too. He wanted Claude Jr. to be named after him, and I could not deny such a loving, proud dad. So we named both of the children I had with Claude after him.

Claude and Claude Jr. loved to go fishing together. They would grab their fishing equipment and off they would go.

Claude and Claude Jr. were fishing. Claude took Angela and Claudanna too.

We took Sammy in for three years, and he was fourteen years old at the time. It was an adjustment for our children because of our lifestyle and what Sammy was used to. We took our family to church and raised them by God's principles. We took them on trips and they especially liked the Galveston trips. Claude, Sammy, and Claude Jr. enjoyed fishing together too.

Family picture: Claude, Danva, Sammy,
Angela, Claudanna and Claude Jr.

Claude and I were getting excited because we were going to the hospital to wait for our first grandchild to be born. This would be our daughter Angela's first baby, and she had already named her Bethany.

When Claude and I were waiting at the hospital for our first grandchild to be born, he decided to walk to the other end of the hall. I thought the nurses would bring Bethany out to where I was waiting, but about the time Claude got to the end of the hall the nurse brought Bethany out at that end. So Claude got to hold our new grandchild Bethany first. I went running down the hall to see them.

Later, we became the proud grandparents of Caleb, Austin, Lauren, Andrea, Tessa, and our first great-grandchild, Aylisa (Bethany's daughter). Being there when they were born was such a joy.

God's biggest blessings are our little ones: our children and grandchildren. They will always be my babies, no matter what their ages may be.

Claude and I saw many miracles and healings. We always read our Bibles the first thing in the morning and the last thing before we went to bed.

Claude walked with a cane and wore a built-up shoe. Bell Helicopter—where he worked—had it made for him. He was prayed for one day at Hurst Assembly of God Church, and God miraculously healed his back. He never wore the built-up shoe or used the cane again. Praise God! We saw the Word of God work. He built parts for helicopters there, and it was his job for thirty-eight years until he retired.

I would go shopping while Claude would wait patiently for me, and he never complained that I took too long. People would even comment about how patient he was. I knew Claude loved me, and this made me appreciate him even more.

Claude would give my music CD to people when he felt led to. He gave a CD to a lady cashier at our bank, and she later told us she was saved by listening to it. They called him "preacher man" at Bell Helicopter because Claude would witness for Jesus and was not ashamed to do it.

We helped co-pastor with Pastors George and Wanda Salazar at Gospel Way Church. Our granddaughter, Bethany, was the worship leader. This was on the north side of Fort Worth, where we had started our lives together forty-four years ago.

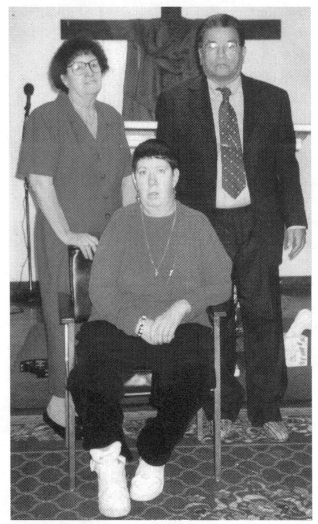

Pastors George and Wanda Salazar, Laura are our precious friends.

We preached and sang, and we all went door-to-door inviting people to church. We saw many people get saved. Even drunk people would come and get sobered up, and then they would get saved.

Claude loved to sing solos of the songs "There Is a River" and "It Is No Secret What God Can Do."

Claude loved and I love Pastor George and Wanda and their daughter, Laura Jane.

Laura Jane was in a wheelchair and was always following Claude around because she loved him too. We were all very close and had many nice times together.

It was something to go back to north side and help with a church for a while. The area has changed a lot since we lived there. The old stockyards that were on the north side have become very famous for tourists now.

One time at Bell Helicopter, a huge piece of steel broke off a machine that Claude was working on and hit him in the stomach. He called out to Jesus. Charley Ray, Claude's coworker, said, "That's right, Claude. Call out to Jesus."

People began to pray for Claude. One man even called his wife and asked her to pray. At that very moment, I was praying at a church. I kept saying, "Many are the afflictions of the righteous, but the Lord delivereth him out of them all." I said that about three times, and I wondered why. I knew it was a Scripture, but I had never memorized it. I found it later in the Bible. It is Psalm 34:19 (KJV).

I knew the Holy Spirit was praying through me for someone. When I got home from church, my phone was ringing. It was Bell Helicopter saying Claude had been hurt.

I raced to the hospital, where doctors told me Claude would not be able to work for months. I told them, "I do not receive that. Jesus will take care of Claude."

That night, I went back to the church to pray. God gave me another Scripture: Psalm 30:5. "Weeping may endure for a night, but joy comes in the morning" (AMP).

The next day, when I arrived at the hospital, Claude's doctors said that X-rays had been taken and they could find nothing wrong with Claude. They sent him home.

Praise God, Jesus had protected and healed him! Claude and I were extremely joyful for this.

Claude and I saw many miracles in our life together. No one can take from me the memories of those times. God was with us, and we depended on His power and anointing to see us through our journey.

Claude, Danva with our 25ᵗʰ Wedding Anniversary Cake.

I know now I can lean on the same principles that Claude and I did together, only now it is me alone who must live and trust God. I intend to do just that.

Our family picture at Claude and Danva 25th Wedding renewal of vows

*Claudanna, Doug, Angela, Beth, Caleb, Claude Jr. Melanie, Danva,
Claude, Austin, Lauren, Jim. With our "Praise the Lord" picture behind us.*

Chapter Three

THE EARLY MORNING OF CLAUDE'S PROMOTION AND THE FUNERAL

THE MORNING CLAUDE WAS PROMOTED TO heaven, I had been baking for Thanksgiving and Claude was waiting up for me.

It was getting late, about one thirty on Thanksgiving morning.

I began to talk to Claude. "I know you like to scrape the bowls after I am through with them," I said. "Here is the bowl I made the banana pudding in." I had left some extra pudding in the bowl for him to eat. I noticed he looked tired.

"It is getting late, and I am not finished yet," I continued. "Go ahead and eat your pudding and go to bed, if you are ready to. There is no sense in us both having to stay up."

Claude asked, "Are you sure you don't want me to wait up with you?"

"No, you go ahead and go to bed," I said. "I know you are tired. And you know me. I always stay up late when I am baking."

Never did I dream that these would be the last words we would say to each other. I wish that I could have foreseen what was about to happen. I would have stopped my baking and gone to bed with him. We would have cuddled up, and I would have told him a million times that I loved him.

I can say right now, "I love you, Claude. I love you, Claude. Loving you was not a sin, and I would do it all over again."

He went to bed, and about an hour later I went to bed. I had been lying down for about thirty minutes when I heard Claude make a funny noise. He did it again, and when I asked him if he was all right he did not respond.

I went around to his side of the bed. "Claude, are you all right?" I asked. He did not respond.

I could see there was something wrong with him, so I began to pray for him. "Father, in the name of Jesus I command the Devil to get his hands off Claude. I submit myself to You, God, and I take my authority in the name of Jesus. I pray for healing in his body for whatever is wrong."

I put on my clothes, turned off my alarm, and called 911. The ambulance arrived at our house in three minutes. The EMTs made me leave the room.

Then I called Claudanna, my daughter, and she said she would be right over. I called Pastor Brenda and Fred Ballinger at Eagle Mountain International Church and asked them to pray. I also called Ken and Sue Hatmaker from EMIC. I asked them to pray, and they met me at the hospital.

The ambulance staff worked on Claude and then said, "We must take him to the hospital immediately." Claudanna and I followed in her car. When we arrived at the hospital, I told them, "I want to be in the room with him, so I can pray for him."

As I began to pray for him, the doctor said, "I have gotten a pulse! I have gotten a pulse!" Then he asked me to leave the room for a minute. When I came back into the room, the doctor told me, "I am sorry, Mrs. York, but your husband has passed."

They had continued to work on Claude. They said they worked on him longer than normal to try to bring him back for me.

I prayed again. "I take my authority over you, devil, and rebuke you off Claude. I command his spirit to come back into his body. I rebuke you spirit of death off him, in the name of Jesus. I claim 1 Peter 2:24 (KJV). By Jesus' stripes, he is healed."

My children were concerned about me, and they told me later that Sue Hatmaker told them I was trying to pray Claude back from the dead—and I was. The nurses were praying with me and patting me.

Then the doctor said again, "I am sorry, Mrs. York. It is over."

I looked up to heaven and said, "Jesus, I love you more than Claude, but I do love Claude with all my heart. If his assignment on this earth is finished, then I accept that."

I knew that in Hebrews 9:27 it says it is appointed unto men once to die. Ecclesiastes 3:1–2 says, for everything there is a season, and a time to every purpose under the heaven, a time to be born and a time to die. I knew also that I could not love anyone more than Jesus.

Oh, how my heart was hurting! As I went outside the hospital room, I began to faint and someone caught me. Then I heard someone say that maybe they should have the doctor give me a shot.

I said, "No! That is what they did to me when Eddie passed." I had a flashback of being in the hospital where Eddie had been, years ago. I began to see myself running again outside that hospital of years ago. But this time, I wanted to be awake.

I hurt so badly that I thought I was going die of a broken heart. I told myself, "Not again. This cannot be real. I have gone through this before."

Then I prayed again. "Oh, my God, help me. It's too hard to carry. The aching and breaking of my heart have been through this before, and I don't want to go there. Take me too, for surely this load is too hard for me to bear."

Inside me, where no one could hear me, I was screaming, I can't endure this again. No! Jesus, no! I can't do this another time. I have borne this earlier in my life. I feel like I'm in a box and I can't get out, and no one can help me.

The numbness set in and fear began to grip me. The thought of being alone again and without Claude was more than I could bear. I had loved my life with Claude. He always made me feel secure. I did not know how I could make it without him.

That day, my family and I were all in shock. My sister Charlotte and my brother Oscar Dale were there to help us when we weren't sure how to take the next step. Oscar Dale went to the store and brought us dozens of eggs and sausage patties, so if we were hungry we would have something to eat. And later that day, Charlotte invited us to Thanksgiving dinner at her home. They all went above and beyond what I could ever ask for or think of.

Angela, Claudanna, Bethany, Andrea, Aylisa, and I went shopping for clothes for the funeral. We were all in a daze. I was sitting down when suddenly Aylisa came to me and said, "Nana, I have a song for Papa."

"Sing it to me, baby," I told her. After she did, I said, "Aylisa, this is a precious song for your papa. Will you sing it at your papa's funeral?"

"Yes, Nana," she said, "I will sing it for you. The name of the song is 'My Papa' because I love him too, Nana." This was a joyful time with my great grandchild.

Claude had given Pastor George a "Jesus" gold belt buckle while we were helping pastor at Gospel Way Church. Pastor George came to the visitation the night before the funeral. He came up to me with tears in his eyes. "Danva," he said, "I would like for you to put the belt buckle in the casket with Claude." It was a special, touching moment.

With tears in my eyes, I replied, "I will do that for you. I know Claude sees your love and friendship." I wish I could have captured that moment on camera.

There were many plants and flowers from Eagle Mountain International Church, Gateway Church, friends, and family. I still have a lot of them, and I gave them to my children.

The funeral was very nice, and it was a wonderful service. His family and coworkers and friends had loved Claude. The friends Claude had worked with at Bell Helicopter stood up and shared stories about him and how they cared about him and what a good domino player he was.

One man shared how Claude had inspired him to become a better husband to his wife.

A nurse from a nursing home where Claude and I ministered also shared about Claude.

Angela, our daughter, read a poem about her dad, and you would never know they were not blood related.

Aylisa, our great granddaughter, sang her precious song "My Papa."

We played my CD of the song "Wind beneath My Wings" and "My Hero." I never dreamed, when I recorded the song "My Hero," that it would be played at Claude's funeral. As I have already shared, right before I married Claude he became my hero. That is why that song was so fitting for Claude.

"A SILVER SETTING" Danva CD that Claude encouraged her to record.

I know Claude was looking down from heaven and was proud of them. All of his children and grandchildren have honored their dad and papa, and I know it touched him.

Anju Chettri is from India, and Claude and I had embraced her as our adopted daughter.

Anju our heart adopted Indian daughter that God gave to us she is unique.

She stayed by my side through everything, just like my own children did. Claude and our entire family have loved her very much. In Anju's country, they do not allow the women to go to funerals, so Claude's funeral was the first one she had ever attended.

We first met Anju at the Hurst Northeast Mall. I had gone there to look for some jewelry that I needed for a fashion show I was planning. When I came up to the store where she was, she approached me and said,

"I saw a cross the other day on a church and I felt so drawn to it. I have never been to a church, only my temple." She said though, "I have been watching Joel Osteen's church service on TV." I told her, "Honey, this was a sign from heaven to you. You were drawn to look at the cross because Jesus wants you to find Him." It was an opened door for me to tell her about Jesus.

She had never met me before that day. I shared with her and asked her, "Would you like to pray with me to accept Jesus into your heart?"

She said, "Yes, I want to pray with you."

I realized this was one of my assignments here on earth, which unfolded as part of my destiny. The evangelist anointing in my life was upon me, and I was excited God used me.

Many people began coming up to look at the jewelry. I asked God, "Please remove these people so I can pray with her." Then, suddenly, the people left.

Anju asked, "Can we pray now?"

I said, "Yes." I told her to repeat the prayer after me, and she did.

Anju said, "Jesus, will you forgive me of my sins? I am sorry for all the things I have done wrong. I repent from them, and I ask you to come into my heart." A great joy came over her, and she looked so happy. We both rejoiced! Anju said, "I have so much peace now."

I replied, "I have the same peace too, and isn't it wonderful? God blessed us today. All of heaven is rejoicing over you today, and so am I."

Anju became close to Claude and me and came to our house often. We started going places together and enjoying each other's company. What a wonderful time that was, watching my beautiful Indian girl when she asked Jesus into her heart. Claude bought Anju a Bible with a cross on it and we claimed her as our daughter.

Disney World had brought Anju to America, to work for them. Later she came to Texas to go to college. God placed her in our lives right after her own father passed in India. She had not been able to go back to India to be with her family after her father's passing.

We knew for certain that God meant for her to become part of our family so we could give her love and comfort.

Now Anju has comforted me. She comes to see me and brings me food, presents, and her love. I am so grateful to God that he brought Anju all the way from India to the American mall where we met. She is a precious young lady, and it was an honor to pray with her and have her in our lives.

When Anju comes to see me, she will eat supper with me and we sit and talk. I enjoy her company so very much. She has been such a comfort to me. I am proud to be her "American mom" and have her as my "Indian daughter."

So many people brought us food and came over to our house to minister to us after Claude died. My grandchildren—Bethany, Caleb, and Austin—stayed at the house to greet the people who were bringing food and to take phone calls. I did not take any phone calls for a while, because I was in a daze. My grandchildren pitched right in to help.

Many other people offered to help me, and I did appreciate it. I was still in a daze and many people were there to support me. If I have not honored you, I do now. Thank you, thank you, from the bottom of my heart.

One couple, Darrell and Barbara Decker, outdid themselves.

Darrell and Barbara Decker they were like angels to my family and I.

They brought food before the funeral and even two months after. They stood by my side and took me out many times—to restaurants, church meetings, shopping, and other places. Darrell and Barbara still call to check on me often. They ministered to me and prayed with me. They told me the Bible says we are to take care of the widows, and they did that royally for me. I knew I could call them and they would be here for me.

The Deckers had David Gardinar at their home, and he ministered to me too. I know God assigned them to me to help me through this time in my life. I do not know what I would have done without Darrell and Barbara.

Ken and Sue Hatmaker, Pastor Brenda Ballinger, Pastor Mary Jo Pierce, Kathy Overton, Carrie Rivers, Norma Chambers, Kathy Jones, Vernon and Patty Perry, Bertie and Gloria Stoneman, and Pastors George and Wanda Salazar were there to help me. Laura Gross, Lori Dugdale, Margaret Canafax, Lillian Mac Leod, Duane and Laura Sanner, Jerry and Becky Lunsford, Jack and Sharon Nowlin, Mike and Sharon Hinkle, Susan Overcash, Danny and Katherine Hubbard, and Duane and Linda Dolney called me, brought food, took me places, and showed their support.

My aunt, Retha Stinson; my cousins, Tommy and Brenda Dodge, John and Betty Cook, Danny and Terry Stinson, David and Terri Stinson, and their families; my nieces, Christy Thomas and her husband Jason, Stephanie Mc Cullough, Wendy Mace, Kim and her husband, Joe Rodriguez; my nephews, Timothy and Robert Eckhart; my brother, Oscar Dale Curington; my sisters, Sherry Matthaei, Barbara Ann Eckhart and her husband Jerry, Nancy Southard, and Charlotte and her husband Gary Yeathermon, Phyllis and her husband Rick Holder; and my grandchildren, Jeremy and Lauren Francis and Steve and Wendy Bennie, sent flowers, cards, books, gifts, and candy and they called me.

Pastor Brenda Ballinger and the Ladies Bible Study at EMIC gave me the books *My Dream of Heaven* and *Sorrow Not*.

Dee Ann Dixon gave me the books *Within Heaven's Gates* and *Sorrow Not*.

The Gateway Home Group leaders, Johnny and Pam Williams, and the home group outdid themselves too. There were two home-goings to heaven in our home group; Claude was first, and then Lee Chambers passed only two days later. The home group was making two of everything. They were putting my name on one bowl and Norma Chambers's on another bowl as they prepared food for us.

Gateway's Mosaic Ministry for Widows has been a blessing to me. It had a brunch at Gateway Church for all widows and treated us like queens. We were served a wonderful brunch. They had beautiful teacups and saucers for us to drink out of and to take home with us, plus gifts for us. In attendance at the brunch, they had about one hundred widows.

Joe and Donna Christ are the Home Group leaders over the Hurst residents who are widows who attend Gateway Church. They plan brunches, outings, and whatever the widows of Gateway Church would need or enjoy. They told us they are available if we need prayer or any kind of help. They have called and prayed for me, and they told me they would be there for me if I needed them.

Joe and Donna are excited for my book to be published and believe my book will minister to the widows and anyone who has lost a loved one.

I felt so blessed to have so many ministers and friends, because of all the things they did for me and my family. There were so many prayers, cards, and phone calls. I pray that I have not left anyone out.

Pastor Terri Copeland Pearsons (Kenneth Copeland's daughter) called and ministered to me and prayed for me on the phone. I took notes because I did not want to forget what she had shared with me. I have included her words of encouragement and prayer later in my book because I want to share them with you. It was such an honor for Terri to call me.

Eagle Mountain International Church is where my daughter, Angela, her husband, Doug, and her children, Caleb and Austin MacLeod, attend. This is where Claude and I were attending church before his promotion.

The Sunday morning after Claude's promotion, Pastors George and Terri Pearsons called Angela's family and me to the altar to pray for us.

I was not there that Sunday; I had to be somewhere else. I was able to watch it later on my computer. Oh, how it touched me! I was grateful they cared about us and prayed for us.

Betty Leslie put stamps in the card she sent to me, so I would have extra stamps for thank-you cards. Everyone continued to call me and check on me. I appreciated it, because I was a basket case for the first two months after Claude was promoted to heaven. I needed everyone through that time, and they were there for me. I am so grateful for everyone who did something for me and my family.

Some people commented to me that they really liked the picture of Claude that I put in the newspaper. Claude wore a white and black hat with matching coat, shirt, and tie. He did look so handsome.

Claude let me go to John Robert Power's Modeling School and Beauty Control School, so I learned a lot about putting clothes together. I dressed us to match most of the time, because it showed others that we were one.

I went to modeling school at night, and Claude would not let me drive there by myself. He would sit in the car until I finished my class. What a patient man he was to let me enjoy what I liked to do. Claude paid for my schooling and never complained. I did many fashion shows for churches and he always escorted the ladies off the stage for me. He assisted me wherever I needed him.

Claude loved me with unconditional love, and I was proud to be his wife. At the funeral, I chose the royal color purple for us to wear. Claude was royalty to me, and he always made me feel like a queen.

Anyone who has lost a loved one needs friends. If you have a friend who is in grief, do not wait for that person to call you and say he needs you. Just offer to help or just show up to mow his lawn, clean, buy groceries, pray with him, or offer to take him places.

A person who is mourning will not call you. I have had people say, "Call me if you need me." That is a hard thing for the grieving person to do, because he does not want to impose on people.

So many people called me and said that they wanted to do something for me. I would tell them something I needed, and they would do it. It was a blessing to me. I would thank them for thinking of me.

It is also just as important for me and others to be thankful. We need to let people know we are very appreciative of whatever they do. My family and I have been blessed by so many people, and we are very grateful.

I visited The Glory Church, which is just down the street from me, one Sunday night. I had known the pastors, Bill and Beverly Earley, for many years, and I also wanted to let them know about Claude.

That night a lady came up to me and told me she had attended my husband's funeral. I asked her how she knew him. She told me she did not know him but that she worked with my daughter-in-love, Melanie York. She told me her name was Susan Whitby and that she was also the worship leader at The Glory Church.

Susan told me the Glory Church had a phone prayer center for its TV program. I told Susan that I had retired from the Daystar Television Prayer Phone Center, where I had worked for six years. Claude had retired and was home by himself. I retired to be home with Claude. I am so glad I did that, because I was able to spend four years with Claude before he was promoted to heaven.

Susan invited me to come and pray on the phones if I ever had an opportunity. I felt in my spirit that I was supposed to help them. I wanted to plant a seed into someone's life, knowing that the Word of God says in Luke 6:38, "Give and it will be given back to you."

I was hurting so much inside that I knew it would help me to pray for other people and for a release in my own life. Every time I went to pray on the phones, I was greatly blessed.

I was also blessed by Pastors Bill and Beverly Earley, Gregory and Sylvia Rosario, and Mary Cantu and Judy Levy, and prayer ministers at the prayer center. They made me feel very welcomed and a part of the ministry.

Praying on the phones again began a healing in my life. I am so grateful for the opportunity to be used and to work side by side with precious people of God.

Since Claude's funeral, I have met so many new people and have begun to do different things. One thing that has not changed though is my time with the Lord in prayer and in the Word of God. I spend most of my morning doing that, and I always have.

My daily routine of life still goes on without Claude here, but I do miss him being with me. We always shared what we read in the Bible. Claude would spend time with the Lord in the mornings too, and at night we would pray together and read our Bibles again. My lifestyle with God will always be first in my day and my life.

I look forward to seeing Claude again. I know he is not dead. He is just away with Jesus in heaven. To be absent from the body is to be present with the Lord. He is not in his body anymore, but his spirit lives forever. The spirit man never dies; only the body does. Knowing this makes me comprehend I am a spirit and I live in a body. I will see Claude again, and you will see your loved ones too.

In Matthew 21:43 (AMP), Jesus said, "The kingdom of God will be taken away from you and given to a people who will produce the fruits of it." I have to live my life for Jesus and accept him as my Savior as I have done, and then produce good fruits for His kingdom, and I will see Claude again.

It is a real commitment, and when you do that you will want to live for Jesus and live a life pleasing to him. Your life will portray the fruits of the spirit. Then you will not want to do anything our precious Father God in heaven would not want you to do.

There is a connection to heaven and to be able to see our loved ones again. It is this simple prayer and a sincere commitment.

Jesus, I ask you to come into my heart and forgive me of all my sins. I believe you died for my sins and rose up from the grave. I know you are interceding for me in heaven. I make you number one in my life, and I accept you as my Lord and as my Savior. Thank You, Jesus for saving my soul. I know now if I am to die tonight that I will go to heaven to be with you.

All stress has to take a flight away from me. Knowing death is only to my body and not to my spirit which is the real me. This hope rises up in me, and I can trust God Almighty to take care of me through all eternity.

Chapter Four

HOW I HAD TO DEAL WITH FEAR

THE FEAR BEGAN AS SOON AS Claude had gone to heaven. For two months, I told my children I did not want to be alone. All of my children and some of my grandchildren stayed with me, when they could, for those two months. They were a blessing.

I tried different ways of dealing with the fear. The fear of being alone was hard to deal with, because for forty-four years I had never been alone. It may seem a small thing to some people, but it wasn't small for me. I had so much grief that it was all I thought about. I was in a daze thinking I would wake up and it would only be a dream.

Until you deal with fear, it will not go away. I kept expecting Claude to come home, but of course he never did. The fear of Claude never coming home again terrified me.

I also had fears about my finances. I had to return Claude's retirement checks until they could put them in my name. For three months, the money I had in my bank account was all that I had to pay my bills. The bank was debiting my account as the bills came due, and the amount I had left in the account went down every day. Fear about this confused me.

One day my grandson, Austin, came into my room and said, "Nana, I am going to give you my savings and I do not want you to pay me back for it."

I said, "Austin, I can't take your money."

He said, "Yes, Nana, God wants me to do this for you." What a blessing that was for me! That money was sufficient until my checks began coming again.

I told my daughter, Angela (who is Austin's mother), that when I pass I want Austin to get back double what he gave me from the inheritance they would get from me. Austin's gift to me immediately removed the fear about my finances. Bless his sweet heart—he obeyed God, and I know God will bless him.

When Austin gave me that money, he was being "seed-minded" for me instead of being "need-minded" for himself. As in Matthew 13:32. I pray his seed to me will become like a tree, and it will come back to him larger than his gift to me.

Austin took pictures of our family and he allowed me to use them in my book. They add a special touch. He has many talents and gifts and I am proud of him.

I had a fear about going places alone. I did not even want to go to church by myself! Angela, my daughter, and Bethany, my granddaughter, took me to church.

Angela and my other daughter, Claudanna, went to the store and bought the groceries and other things I needed for the house. They also put gas in my car so I didn't have to spend money for any of those things. They took over, because I was a basket case. I do not know what I would have done without them.

Melanie, my daughter-in-love, helped me with insurance issues—because the day Claude went to heaven, my health insurance was canceled. I was in good health, which was a good thing.

My son, Claude Jr., bought me a new Sparkletts water cooler because my old cooler was not getting cold anymore. He also started buying my water. He repainted my swing for me, and now it looks new. He also put new locks on things so I would have one key to everything.

Claude Jr. told me that his dad had talked with him about what to do if anything ever happened to him. Claude Jr. said he would be taking care of whatever I needed around the house that I could not do myself. He said he would still mow the lawn as he had already been doing for his dad. What a blessing that was, because I have never mowed.

Bethany took care of all my phone calls, because I did not use the phone that much. My grandsons, Caleb and Austin, would do whatever else needed to be done around the house.

Even after they had gone back to their home, I would call Bethany sometimes because I could not stop crying. Bethany, Caleb, and Austin would come right over and stay with me. Their families were gracious to let me borrow them for a time. What a blessing they all were to me! I can say my children and my grandchildren stood by me until I could stand on my own again.

When there was no one here, sometimes I would frantically start crying. Then I would call Angela, and she would come back to stay with me until I calmed down.

Claudanna knew that I was not cooking for myself, so she and her husband, Jim, began cooking food every week to bring to me. They also took me out to eat many times and sometimes brought me to their house to eat and spend the night with them.

Jim set up my computer. He still helps me on the computer when I need him to—he even put the computer on a surge protector. He does my GPS map updates and he amazes me with all he knows about the computer and other things.

Andrea, my granddaughter, made my bed, brought me a lamp, and got me an electric blanket because I used one at my home and she wanted me to be comfortable. They were all so sweet and caring to me.

One day, my electricity went off when I was by myself. I called Claude Jr. who came and took me to his house to spend the night. He cooked us a steak and Melanie fixed us salad and potatoes. Everything tasted so good. Tessa, my granddaughter, brought me some ice cream and we enjoyed every spoonful of it.

Tessa tried to comfort me and look after me as if she was the Nana and I was her granddaughter. Melanie made my bed, and I felt so secure because I did not have to go home to a dark house.

I am so blessed to have my wonderful children and grandchildren! "Children are a heritage of the Lord and a gift from God" (Psalm 127:3 AMP).

Our precious children with Howard and me:
Claude Jr. Angela, Danva, Howard and Claudanna at Christmas 2011.

Our precious grandchildren with Howard and me:
Austin, Bethany, Caleb, Jeremy, Lauren, Danva,
Howard, Andrea, Aylisa and Tessa.

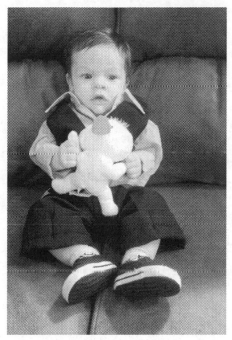

Dorian our precious great grandson in his Easter clothes we bought him.

Our children and grandchildren are a crowning glory to us, their parents, and grandparents. When I say my children, which includes my daughter-in-love and my sons-in-love. I call them all my children. They are all a blessing to me.

I began to have fear about driving, especially driving at night by myself. I did not trust my car, so I had to deal with that. For the first two months, I did not drive unless I had to. My children and grandchildren did most of the driving. I planned to buy a new car when I received the life insurance money.

I had fear about putting gas in my car because Claude had always done that. I just panicked about everything. There were many things that I did not know how to do around the house, and I was fearful about them.

One day, Caleb took me to the gas station to teach me how to put gas in my car. It was not as bad as I thought it would be, but I still wanted someone to go with me to get gas until I felt I could do it alone.

On the way home, Caleb asked me, "Nana, are you still having fear about being alone?"

I answered, "Yes, I am."

Caleb shared with me how he dealt with fear. His brother, Austin, was sick and he was afraid he would become sick too.

Angela, Caleb's mom, told him to write out 2 Timothy 1:7 (KJV). "For God has not given us the spirit of fear, but of power and of love and of a sound mind."

Angela told Caleb to read it out loud over and over until the fear left him. Caleb said he did that and the fear did leave him.

I told Caleb, "You are going to be a preacher, and I really needed this sermon tonight!"

When we got home, we had a good laugh. Caleb said to his mom, "Mom, you should have seen Nana at the gas station. It was hilarious! Nana had her purse on her arm, her cell phone and gas card in one hand, and the gas handle in the other hand. She was trying to hold all those things and put the gas in her car. I told her, 'Nana, why don't you put your purse and phone back in the car? It would be easier for you.' "Nana said, 'Because I don't want anyone to get my things.'"

Caleb continued the story. "I said, 'Just lock your car up and only keep your keys and gas card.'"

That moment hit us as funny, and we laughed and laughed. This was God giving me joy and a special time with my sweet grandson.

I replied, "Caleb, I think you are right, and that is a good idea." Needless to say, I had never put gas in a car. I can now breeze through putting gas in my car because I had a good teacher.

I realized that I was going to have to deal with the spirit of fear coming against me. I knew that, but I was in so much grief that I wasn't taking my authority over the Devil. I was letting the spirit of fear attack me.

I knew I was going to have to send my children and grandchildren back to their families and homes so that I could deal with fear on my own. One day, I decided that this was the day to send them home.

I began to confess 2 Timothy 1:7 (KJV), and I typed it then put copies around my house. When I would walk by wherever I had put the Scripture, I would confess it aloud. The power of confessing the Word of God is so mighty and authoritative. I have done this every morning for years in my prayer time. I just had to hold onto my confession, even if I was missing Claude.

On the wall next to my bed, I hung a big, framed Scripture with a cross at the bottom. It says, "Hope, fear not, for I am with you. Be not dismayed, for I am your God. I will strengthen you, yes, I will help you. I will uphold you with the right hand of my righteousness" (Isaiah 41:10 (NIV).

I confessed this Scripture every time I passed by it and before I went to bed at night. I knew I was going to have to do spiritual warfare, but now I was ready.

That doesn't mean I didn't call my children crying and saying, "It is so hard and I miss your dad so much. I want him to come back to me." I knew he could not come back, because it would only be a familiar spirit. I am so glad I had the wisdom to realize that, because I no longer needed to fear.

I believe that my saying "I want your dad to come back" brought an ordeal that I faced one night. In the middle of the night, I woke up and I couldn't move. I heard Claude's voice talking to me, but I could not understand the voice. I saw a figure, and I said, "I cannot move."

I realized it was a spirit of fear trying to come against me.

I screamed, "I rebuke you, spirit of fear!" I heard something stomp upstairs. I knew it was a familiar spirit and it was mad because I had discerned what it was. I knew it was not Claude but a familiar spirit.

I went through my house and anointed it with oil, and I commanded every evil spirit to leave my house. I pleaded the blood of Jesus and I asked God to release His angels around me.

My advice is never to want someone to come back if they have already passed. I believe it is all right to talk to your loved ones, but don't allow it to go to the point that you believe that they can appear to you and that you can really have a conversation with them.

They are not in their earthly bodies anymore; they are in their spiritual bodies, which we cannot see. The exception to that would be if you saw them in a dream or a vision.

I know Claude is watching over me now like an angel, but he cannot appear to me in a physical body.

I still have a relationship with Claude, but it is a different one. I talk to him just the way I talk to Jesus. Pastor Terri Pearsons told me to do that, and that has really helped me.

Each of us has a spirit, soul, and body. Claude is in his spiritual body now. He is not dead—he is just away.

Angela suggested that I keep praise music going at night. I did that, and it does make a home feel peaceful.

I knew that the grieving process was necessary to let me heal. I went on a sabbatical seeking God.

I began to have a desire to write a book about being widowed. Every time I would start to write a part of this book, I would take my anointing oil and anoint my forehead, my lips, my fingers, and my hands. I always asked God to help me. I would say, as in Psalm 45:1 (AMP), that my heart will overflow with a goodly theme and that my tongue is like the pen of a ready writer.

I began to write down my thoughts. Later, I would sort them out and decide where I felt they would fit in the book.

As I continued to write, God gave me the names of the chapters. Creating the book has been a process of collecting my thoughts, and it is excellent therapy for me.

God told me, "Danva, you are mine twice. The first time is because I made you. The second time is because I bought you. I am your husband now. I will give you a joyful heart to sing, make melody, and praise me."

Chapter Five

I Began to Rebuild the Walls in My Life

I FACED FEAR, GRIEF, ABANDONMENT, AND LONELINESS. I worried about my children and the big loss in our lives. I knew I had to take control of my life and not let all of this defeat me. I took the Word of God and began to apply it to my situation.

I began to read the book of Nehemiah in the Bible. I call it my "miracle book" of the Bible, because it did catapult and propel me to go forward in my life and be set free.

In Nehemiah 1:3–4 and 2:17–18, 20 (AMP), Nehemiah heard that the walls of Jerusalem had broken down. He sat down and wept and mourned for days. He fasted and prayed constantly before the God of heaven. This is what I did after Claude was promoted to heaven. I sat down and wept for days and fasted and prayed, and I worshiped God.

The walls in my life were broken down. I had loved my husband very much for forty-four years, and now I miss him. I was dealing with the spirit of fear, but I had to rebuild the walls in my life. Sometimes, to my mind came thoughts that I would not succeed in rebuilding those walls—that my life was over for me. I had to rebuke those thoughts in the name of Jesus.

I would rather take the clear road with God than the dark road with the Devil. Pastor Terri Copeland Pearsons had told me not to go down to a dark place. I had to pray to God and trust Him to keep watch over my situation.

I continued to read Nehemiah 6:9, 15–16, and I began to talk to God. "Please, God, strengthen my hands. Help me to rebuild the walls in my life, as they did in these verses. I cry out to you, help me!" It all seemed so unbearable. I think losing a loved one was the hardest thing in my life I have ever faced.

"God," I would say, "I am going to sing this song 'For God Has Not Given Me the Spirit of Fear' and I'm going to believe the words as I sing them. Singing it will give me peace. I am going to do whatever I hear you tell me."

One day, I had an impression to read the book *Sorrow Not* by Kenneth Copeland. This book was a blessing for me, but I was still hurting. I still had to go to the next step, even as I thought, *I cannot go on. It hurts too much.*

One day, I called Angela crying and said, "I cannot go on." She was at work and she called Bethany. She asked her to call the Kenneth Copeland Ministries.

Rebecca Milstine at Kenneth Copeland's called me and prayed with me. Rebecca told me to write a letter to God about all my feelings, my crying, and how much I missed my husband. Then she said for me to cast all my cares on God, as it says in the Scripture 1 Peter 5:7.

She told me to read a few pages of the book *Sorrow Not* every day. As I read it daily, it began to give me hope and courage to resist the unhappy feelings that plagued me.

I had to collect my thoughts and deal with them, and I had to seek the Lord just as it says in Zephaniah 2:1, 3. I wrote a letter to God, and then I cast all my cares on Him. Immediate deliverance took place in my heart and mind. I felt the spirit of fear leave me.

It is so true, as it says in Psalm 34:4, "that God will deliver me from all my fears." He did. Soon, I felt the birthing of a spirit of joy and peace inside me. The Scripture says in Psalm 45:7 and Hebrews 1:9, "God will anoint you with the oil of joy and gladness." I could never have made that happen.

I can say now that it is so much easier to have joy than to have sorrow and all the pain that goes with it. I do not want to go back. It hurts too much. Joy does not hurt. What a revelation in my life that I can now share this news with others—especially with those who will read my book.

I am not saying that I never cry anymore, but now I don't cry all day long.

Tonja Wells from Gateway gave me some Scriptures on widows that also encouraged me. Tonja had been widowed too, a few years earlier, so she knew what I was going through. I began to look up Scriptures concerning widows.

There are so many encouraging Scriptures in God's Word. He gave me insight into how to rebuild the walls in my life, and that insight gave me the ability to teach others. At my meetings were widows who told me they had never gotten over the death of their spouses. One lady said her husband had been gone twelve years and she was still grieving.

I pray that what I have taught and written in my book will comfort all those whose loved ones have been promoted to heaven. I gave copies of the Scriptures about widows to everyone. I claim all of the Scriptures on widows, especially Isaiah 54:5 (NMR), which says, "For my Maker, God, is my husband."

God is my husband now, and it is such an honor to be in the place where God is my husband, protector, provider, comforter, love, joy, and peace. My hope is in God my Maker, knowing He created me for His plan as it pleases Him.

I began singing the song, "The Joy of the Lord Is Your Strength." That is what it says in Nehemiah 8:10–11. When I sang this, it brought me joy. As I sang "be still, for this day is holy, and I will not be grieved and sad," comfort flooded my soul.

As I bowed down to God and worshipped Him, I could feel God's presence. The people in the book of Nehemiah read from the book of the law of God, distinctly, faithfully, so that everyone would understand. When I read from the Bible, it builds my faith just as it did for the people then.

Reading in Nehemiah taught me to trust God to help me rebuild my walls. Romans 10:17 (NMR) says, "Faith comes by hearing and hearing by the Word of God." It became my Nehemiah miracle to reclaim my life and learn to depend on God's enabling power to help me overcome.

One Sunday evening, I was visiting The Glory Church. Judy Levy came to me and walked me to the altar. We walked back and forth, praying, and Judy encouraged me. She said, "Danva, I want to share with you the Scripture 2 Corinthians 1:3–4."

I clung to those verses. What a revelation to me that only God could be the source of my comfort! I was so glad Judy pointed out those Scriptures to me, because they blessed me.

God is the source of my comfort. I think of what I have been through as a mountain I have climbed. My mountain will enable me to help someone else.

On another Sunday evening at The Glory Church, Susan Whitby came off the stage where she was leading worship. She came to me and took my hand and led me to the altar. We began dancing before the Lord and felt His presence. These ladies and many others at The Glory Church were such a blessing to me. I appreciate all of their love and concern for me.

Writing this book has been good therapy. I have cried a lot of tears while writing, but I also claimed my tongue functions like the pen of a ready writer—and it has been. I think writing has helped me heal. Keeping everything inside would not be healing to me. You cannot stuff your grief. You have to surrender grief and send it away from you. Send it back to the footstool of Jesus. Then let joy come to you.

I know letting it out has been better for me, even though it hurt sometimes as the memories arose. I would remember all of the wonderful times we had together.

Sometimes, I would hear a song on the radio and it would touch me. I would ask Angela and Bethany to find the lyrics and music for me. I love music. It helps so much to heal my heart as I begin a new chapter in my life.

The lyrics to these inspirational songs are written by people who are hearing from God and telling His message so that they can minister to someone else who is in need of His healing hand.

It is important for us to help others who are going through the same challenges we have overcome. I can see somewhere down the road the valley that I have gone through. This will help others see a way out. This conquered mountain of grief will enable me to help someone else.

I love the Word of God, and listening to songs about the Word of God gave me even more healing. I want to share two songs from the Word of God that were my lifeline many times. I would sing them even if I did not feel like singing. I would sing them over and over until I got a release of joy in my spirit.

Here are the two songs from the Word of God.

"God Has Not Given Me the Spirit of Fear" from 2 Timothy 1:7 (KJV)

For God has not given me a spirit of fear, but of power and of love and of a sound mind.

So I won't be afraid anymore. He'll be here to hear my prayer every time.

For God has not given me a spirit of fear, but of power and of love and of a sound mind.

So I won't be afraid anymore. He'll be here to hear my prayer every time.

"For the Joy of the Lord Is My Strength" from Nehemiah 8:10–11 (AMP)

The joy of the Lord is my strength. This day is holy to my Lord.

I will not be grieved, I will not be depressed.

For the joy of the Lord is my strength and stronghold.

I will be still, for this day is holy to my Lord.

I will not be grieved and sad, but I will shout for joy.

I will rebuild the walls in my life with the help of my Lord.

For the joy of the Lord is my strength, for the joy of the Lord is my strength.

Chapter Six

Sharing Claude's Belongings with My Children and Grandchildren

THE LAST MONTH THAT MY CHILDREN and some of my grandchildren stayed with me, I decided to share Claude's things. I didn't want to make them wait until I go to heaven.

I know many people want to hold onto those precious possessions, and I understand that. I did keep some things, but I also shared. It was wonderful watching each face light up when they received something they had wanted that had belonged to their dad or papa.

I started with Claude's clothes. Claude Jr., my son, and Caleb and Austin, my grandsons, had a good laugh and had fun trying on everything and modeling them for me. I had a fashion show in my own home, and I loved it! I do enjoy seeing people happy and wearing clothes that complement their good looks.

I knew Claude was looking down from heaven and enjoying the fashion show too. That evening lifted my spirit, because I had been missing Claude so very much and it felt wonderful to laugh and have fun. Sometimes, something wouldn't look good on them and we would all get a good laugh.

Claude had owned a collection of knives, and I let them divide the knives among themselves. I kept the ones I wanted. I left those knives in his knife cabinet that Charlotte had given to us. I put his wedding ring and other precious things in there too. I know the knives were worth a lot of money. You can't put a price on the joy I saw in my family members' faces when I was giving the knives to them.

Claude also had a big collection of hats, and everyone took the hats of their choice. I kept the hats that said, "Jesus Is My Boss, I Love You Jesus, Oklahoma" (where we were married), "Galveston" (where we went on our honeymoon), "Being a Father Was Good—Being a Papa Is Grand," "Case Knives," "Dallas Cowboys," and regular cowboy hats.

Anyone could tell that Claude loved Jesus and was not ashamed of his Lord Jesus.

He had worn all of his hats proudly. He had a special room where he kept his hats. Now I keep Claude's things in his special room. I go in there and memories flood my soul. And yes, I do cry sometimes, but it delights me to see his things. They give me something I can hold onto, and that gives me such comfort.

God made tears to release things in us, so we would not have to keep them all bottled up inside. Now I shed tears when something touches me and not because I am sad. I don't cry all day anymore.

As you can see, Claude was a collector of many things. He also had a collection of watches. I let the boys divide the watches, and I kept some for myself. Amazingly, they never disagreed with each other. If one would admire a watch that another one had chosen, that young man would say, "You take it."

I wanted to keep the watch Bell Helicopter had awarded Claude for thirty-five years of service. I knew he had just put a new battery in it, so I decided to give it to Claude Jr. to enjoy.

Everything that was left, I put back into Claude's beautiful knife cabinet. Charlotte had brought it to America from England. It has a beautiful glass door and sides, and it made a great knife cabinet for Claude. These things will belong to my daughters, because they were not up to going through the knives.

Sharing Claude's belongings was a fun time for the boys. I enjoyed watching them pick and choose. I did give my daughters other things I knew they would want, and they accepted them.

Claude had collected flashlights and ink pens, so everyone was able to choose something that they liked. The flashlights have come in handy for me, and I am glad he had so many. He had big flashlights, middle-sized ones, small ones, and tiny ones. The grandchildren had fun going through all kinds of ink pens he had collected over the years.

Claude had many glasses and sunglasses, so I was able to share those with everyone. I kept a set of gold-rimmed glasses. I keep them on a shelf in my kitchen. When I pass by, I remember my sweet Claude and his golden smile and beautiful brown eyes.

He had special chairs that he sat in, especially his rocking chairs. I even have a picture of him sitting in a rocking chair outside a souvenir shop while we were on our last Galveston vacation.

Claude sitting in a rocking chair at a souvenir shop in Galveston, Texas

Claude had a rocker near our front door and a rocker on our screened-in back porch.

Every time I go by his chairs or rockers, I pause and kiss the chair back where Claude's head once rested. I feel like I am getting a hug from him, and I feel his presence. I can reminisce about all the times he would sit there and we would talk and he would share things with me.

Claude had a swing outside on our front porch, and he loved to swing in it. Everyone in the neighborhood would comment to me, "I saw Claude swinging today." That was one of his favorite pastimes. Patty, my next-door neighbor, told me that she would always remember Claude waiting for the mailman while swinging in his porch swing.

I have to say I think I have the best neighbors on my street. They are always there for me when I need them. I feel safe knowing that they are all around me and looking out for me.

Knowing that Vernon and Patty Perry are next door makes me feel so secure. They said I could call them anytime, day or night, if I needed them. We have lived next door to each other for thirty years.

Before I bought my generator, Vernon would bring us extension cords to plug into his generator when the electricity went off. What a blessing to have lights back on and to know our food would not spoil! After Claude was promoted to heaven, Patty brought me things to eat, and that was a blessing. I was not cooking or eating right, because I was grieving and did not care to cook.

Ann Grammer is my neighbor two houses from me. Her husband went to heaven before Claude. She shared with me how she still misses her husband. When I taught at a ladies' meeting about how I was rebuilding my walls, Ann came to hear me speak. We have both shared the same loss, and we have tried to comfort each other.

Anna Lopez lives across the street from me. Anna told me that when she gets up early for work, she looks from her house to check on mine. She says she checks on the other neighbors' houses too. One day, I brought Claude's Spanish coins over to Anna's house and she told me what the different coins were. It is good to have neighbors you can talk with too.

One day, I bought a clock radio, but I couldn't get it out of the box because the screws were too tight. I went outside and saw Anna talking to

Terry Jones. Terry is a neighbor who lives next door to Anna. I asked him if he could take the screws out and, with Anna cheering him on, Terry got them out. My neighbors have been there for me, and I do appreciate them all.

Claude enjoyed our neighbors. I'm sure he is pleased with how they have looked after me.

Chapter Seven

LEARNING TO DO THINGS I HAD NEVER DONE BEFORE

CLAUDE HAD SPOILED ME. HE DID so many things that I didn't have to do and never had done. I was completely devastated when I became aware that there were so many things I knew nothing about. I had to learn how to do the things Claude had done on a daily basis.

Claude had his chores, and I had mine. We did share some things, but our habit was that I did mine and he did his. Since now I had to do them all, I knew I was going to have to acquire knowledge quickly. Thanks to my family, I learned to do most things, but I'm still in the process of learning more.

The process of becoming strong like an eagle has become my theme. I am glad that I can stand alone—with Jesus to help me—and be confident to go forward, taking one day at a time.

On my fortieth birthday, my sister Charlotte gave me an album with the song "One Day at a Time" on it. I included this song on the first record album that I recorded.

A friend of mine who is also a singer, Jesse Segura, made a Spanish mariachi music CD sound track of this song for me. Now I can sing this song with the Spanish version of the music, and it blesses me. I have this song in my spirit, and I have done what it says. I take one day at a time. This has become a guideline for me.

I thank my sister Charlotte for being led to give me that album. She didn't know that, years later, I would use the theme of that song and take one day at a time to become strong like an eagle. This did help me to go on with my life without my precious husband.

While my children were staying with me, one of them said, "Mom, did you get your mail today?"

I said, "No, your dad always got the mail. I am not in the habit of going to the mailbox, so I forgot."

They insisted that I go get the mail, but I found I could not open the mailbox because it was too hard for me. Sometimes after that, they would go get the mail for me and they'd tease me, saying, "Oh, Mom, you're just not strong enough!"

My son-in-love, Doug, went out to check the mailbox for me once, and when he tried to open it, the lock broke! Something had been wrong with it. Doug took the lock to the locksmith and had a new one made. Needless to say, I remember to get my mail now, and I have accomplished another thing.

By the way, the lock was beginning to break—of course it happened only to me. When the lock wouldn't turn, muscleman Doug twisted the key off. This proves maybe Mom is not so weak after all. Goody for me and I love it love it. Ha!

I had never changed the filter on our heater or air conditioner, so Doug and Caleb taught me how to do that. I took a red marker and marked the correct way to put it in. Praise God! That was another accomplishment for me, and I know I have more to come.

Doug and Caleb, as I shared before, taught me how to put gas in my car. For all the years I had driven a car, I had never put in gas because Claude always did that for me. I think everyone should learn how to put gas in their cars. I became stressed out about not knowing how, but since I have learned to do it I found it is not hard at all. That was one more accomplishment for me, and it felt good.

I never had put light bulbs in our yard lights before, but Claude Jr. taught me how to do that. I can say, officially, that I have learned to do that chore well. I even know how to wiggle them if they go off when the bulb is still good.

Since I had never taken out the trash, I did not even know the day it was picked up on our street. So I found out, and I wrote myself a reminder. I began to remember, *Oh, today I put out the trash.*

Claude was very independent. He preferred to do his chores himself. I believe he had the gift of helping and a servant's heart. He always set my alarm clock for me, but now I had to set it myself. I just had to get into the routine of doing things I had never done before. Each time I did, it was another accomplishment for me.

I know these things may seem simple to someone else, but if you have never done them before, you just have to learn. My new accomplishments were adding up. I was beginning to feel more independent at last.

Doug, Caleb, and Austin changed all my clocks when the time changed and put new batteries in the ones that needed them. Since then, I have had to change some batteries—and I did it. Hurrah! That was one more thing I learned. It is amazing to me all the little things I didn't know how to do, but now I do. When you are going through grief and having to learn things too, it can be overwhelming. Praise God, I did persevere and learned to do a lot of new things.

When my electricity went off, I decided to buy a generator. Claude Jr. taught me how to use it. I took notes and typed them up. He is a good teacher, and he made me go over and over the procedure until he was sure I knew how to do it. I keep my notes close to my back porch, which is where Claude Jr. put the generator, along with one of Claude's big flashlights. This is a very handy place for them to be in case the power goes off at night. Good idea!

Bethany taught me how to record a program on U-verse for times when I want to see something but am not able to be at home when it is playing. I think that is so neat, and I appreciate her so much. She is such a precious granddaughter.

Angela bought me a flash drive for Mother's Day so I could store my book on it, and that was a good thing because my computer crashed soon after. Angela and Bethany taught me how to use the flash drive, which was another new thing for me to learn. I never knew I would use my computer as much as I have lately. I think it is so neat to be able to store my book on my flash drive.

Lena Dooley, my first editor, told me it would even be more secure to get a hard drive to work on for my book. I did buy one at Office Depot, and I am amazed at the kind people who helped me at this particular store: Rory Day, Dustin Pike, Zackery Wood, Heather Piper, Julia Bright, Mary Endicott, Daniel Digiovanni, Katie Echels, Bill Whitfill, and Kathryn Applin. They have become my friends, and what a blessing they have been to me. I had many projects on my book they helped me with: computer issues and supplies as well as making my sample books, sample cover, and copies. They even took the time to teach me things I needed to learn on my computer to enhance my project. They took time out for me beyond the normal.

Sometimes, when I would go to the refrigerator to get something to eat, I would find that it had spoiled. I realized that I had to buy food in smaller quantities now. It is so different cooking for one person compared to cooking for two.

I do not cook for myself as much as when I had to cook for both of us; instead, I just go to the grocery store and buy something from the deli. I do try to eat as healthy as I can. On Mother's Day, Claudanna bought some buffalo meat for me at Whole Foods, and my son-in-love, Jim, cooked it for me on his grill. It tasted very good! They let me take what I didn't finish eating home with me. Claude and I were the only ones in our family who would eat buffalo meat. It is very nutritious, and I enjoy it.

One day, I decided I wanted to mow my own lawn because Claude Jr. was unable to come. I tried to use the lawnmower that I have, but it seemed hopeless because I was not strong enough to start it. I decided to call Howard Meister from church, because he had offered to help me if I ever needed him. He came over, looked at the lawn mower, started it, and then said, "This mower is fine. It's actually better than the one I have at home. The only problem is you will have to push it yourself because the self-propelled belt is broken. I will buy one and fix it for you."

Howard and my fixed lawnmower and he is a good friend to me.

Howard also taught me how to put gas in the mower, work the choke, hold the handle, and pull the starter. I took notes, and he instructed me to practice it again and again. The next day, I mowed the front yard and part of the back. Success! But suddenly the lawn mower quit working.

When I went into the house, I noticed my face looked like a red beet. It was very hot outside. I called Howard and told him the mower wouldn't start, and he said he would come over to see what the problem was. He called me outside. "Danva, I want you to do something. Take off the gas cap and look down into the gas tank. Tell me, what do you see?"

I said, "Oh, my goodness, there is no gas in there!"

We laughed so much, and he asked if he could share my experience with our friends at the church. I agreed, because it was so funny. The laugh released me from deep mourning and filled me with joy.

Needless to say, the lawnmower was a good one. I used all the gasoline mowing just one time, because I had not properly filled it up the first time. I couldn't believe the gas was all gone, but I must admit I was very thorough when I did that mowing so no sprigs of grass would pop up.

The very hardest thing I have had to learn to do is to be alone, because Claude was always with me. I loved him with all my heart. When I go to bed at night and see his side of the bed empty, I miss him so much. I keep one of his pajamas tops on his side of our bed, and I hold it until I go to sleep.

When I make the bed every morning, I hug the stuffed animals he bought for me and then put them on his side of the bed. Claude once gave me a love note attached to the big teddy bear. It makes me feel like I am getting a hug from him.

Stuffed animals, Claude gifts to me with his picture and he was a gift to me.

I am only sharing what I do because maybe someday it will help someone else who loses a loved one. Some people say I should put everything of his away so I can get over missing him. But I say, "No. Walk through your hurt and enjoy the memories of your loved one."

There is love all around in my home, left to me by Claude, and I find myself feeling grateful when I remember.

*Claude playing his new guitar and I am sure
he is playing a guitar in heaven.*

I say this every day: "Jesus, help me remember that nothing's going to happen to me today that you and I can't handle together. I know all things work together for good to those who love God" (Romans 8:28).

All the things that I have done or have been through in the past were only preparations for what I am going to do. The greatest things and the things that will bring the most glory to God are yet to be revealed to me and yet to be done. I know God is preparing my heart so I will not doubt when He speaks.

I will not worry about tomorrow, because I know God is already there. God knows the plans He has for me, plans to prosper me and not to harm me, plans to give me hope and a future. My calling is just beginning. I will learn to do the things that God has planned for me to do.

Chapter Eight

THE BEAUTY OF GOD'S NATURE AND BIRDS

Yellow birds painted by my Mother, Dorothy Curington. I miss you Mother!

Birds have always had a part in my prayer time. When I go upstairs to pray in my prayer room, I sit by the big window so I can see the birds and look up to God. I have prayed many prayers by that window, especially for my children when they still lived at home.

I would often see a red bird come and sit on the fence when I needed an answer to my prayer. To me, this was God's confirmation that He had heard me.

I love watching the birds as the sun rises in the morning. There would be all kinds of them, and in great numbers. Genesis 1:21 shows God has created every bird of the air. It is a beautiful sight, and I love the nature of it all.

The birds of the air come and find shelter in the branches of the trees, as in Matthew 13:32. Some of them come close to my window while others fly through the trees, the sky, and around the houses. Many just perch on the fences.

Upstairs gives me a great view of all of them as they start their busy days—just as we humans do. The only difference is that they don't seem to have a care. They just do what God created them to do.

When we had a back screened-in porch made, I hung red birds all around the top of it. So you can see they are a part of my life.

When I was nine years old, my sisters and I lived in a two-story house and we had a pet bird. Our little bird's wings had been clipped so he could not fly. He would hop up and down the stairs, and he was so cute. We received so much enjoyment from our little bird.

I still love watching birds. They are so tiny, but they survive—and that means I can survive, and so can you, no matter what we face. God's eye is on the sparrow and He watches over you and me.

You may be wondering why I am writing about birds. I am going to tell you. There was a prophetic word given to me on August 27, 2010, by Prophet David Gardiner.

The word was that the Lord was going to be speaking to me through nature, through some birds. The birds would come and sing new songs. The Lord was going to speak deep things to me, and I would feel the anointing of the Holy Spirit when the birds came and started singing. I would receive waves of joy, waves of joy, and waves of joy.

The birds have come already to me and have been singing, so this word is confirmation from God. When I came home from the meeting at Darrell and Barbara Decker's house, where Prophet David had spoken these words over me, I remembered that I hadn't taken my mail out of the mailbox that day. When I opened my mailbox and looked down, I saw a small package; it had two beautiful red birds on it. I said, "Oh, how beautiful!" and opened the envelope on top. To my amazement, there was a card and a music CD with a big beautiful red bird on it inside. The CD was called *Heaven and Nature Sing!* It was a confirmation down to the last part of my day!

I can say that my loving God spoke to me that day. God used the Paralyzed Veterans of America to send me the confirmation. The birds of the heavens have their nests and they sing, as in Psalm 104:12.

God can speak to us through a bird, a song, a sermon, a person, or a book—so we need to be good listeners. Remember our ears are our faith gates. Our belief system is through our ears. As we pray and speak the Word of God over ourselves and others, we are feeding our spirit. Faith comes by hearing and hearing by the Word of God.

I let the Word of God get into my spirit by praying and speaking the Word out loud.

When you get the Word of God on the inside, it will come out on the outside. When you pray the Word of God every day, it will get into your spirit. Like a computer, whatever Scripture you need will come up in your spirit and then you can pray it over whatever need there is. You do not have to memorize the Word—just pray it over your requests.

Just like the birds trust God to feed and provide for them, we can trust God to provide for us too.

One day, a bird was sitting on the edge of my roof as I came out my front door. The bird began to sing and sing. It was as in Song of Solomon 2:12, which says, "The time of the singing of birds has come."

I looked up to the bird and I asked it, "Are you Claude?" The bird just kept on singing. "You are blessing me so much. I know you were sent from heaven to sing to me," I told the birds. "If you are not Claude singing, please go tell him I love him and I miss him. Tell him I know he is enjoying singing in the choir of heaven."

This happened after Prophet David prophesied over me. It was just a confirmation that David did hear from God, and it was a word for me.

Our human mind can dwell on one thought and then move rapidly to another thought. Sometimes, when I am doing various tasks simultaneously,

I compare this with birds flying in the air rapidly from one place to another place. They are trusting in their Creator to take care of them. That is why I titled my book *Texas Woman Widowed Twice and Becoming an Eagle*. All the creatures of the air fly with the ability that God has given to them. I will continue my life with the ability that God gives me. Claude and I always prayed this: "I take my authority, and it's your ability, God, that you have given me as I pray over this situation today."

That is why I knew in the emergency room—when I took my authority and prayed for Claude to live but He went to heaven—that this happened only because he had fulfilled his assignment here on earth.

This evening when I went to get my mail, I looked up to heaven and said, "Hi, Claude. I miss you." Suddenly the birds in the trees started singing! It sounded just like they were saying, "See you. See you!" Wow! That was so amazing. They sang it perfectly. Pairs of birds flew over my head, and then they became quiet.

This was another confirmation of the prophecy over me. I was enjoying this. It was fun!

I remember one day that Claude and I went to Colleen's house. She raised birds and we wanted to buy one from her. As we went into her house, she asked us to take off our shoes. I assumed she was like me and liked her house clean. She led us into this room, and—my goodness!—I had never seen so many birds up close! The reason we had to take off our shoes was so we would not step on them.

She raised birds to sell and also kept some for herself. She trained them to do many things. She told us, "The ones that like you will come and sit on your shoulder." We had birds flying all above our heads. When we sat down and became still, a yellow bird and a blue bird came and sat on our shoulders.

That was a great experience. We bought both birds. Out of all the birds in that room, these two little parakeets had chosen us to become their human parents. The yellow parakeet came to me and the blue parakeet went to Claude. We felt honored that they chose us.

The eagle is a bird that flies alone and seems to be very content. I have had to adjust my life like an eagle. I am alone a lot, but Jesus never leaves me. I know He is with me even if I have no one else with me. I have come to depend on Jesus more than I ever had before in my whole life.

I know I can't live in the past, and I am supposed to press on to the future. I do enjoy good company, but when I am alone I turn my focus to nature. I will go outside, in my front or backyard, to look at nature. I just watch and draw from the simplicity of the best things in life that are free to admire.

Nature is so calming to your spirit. It shows God's creation and His prized possessions that He created for us to enjoy.

It is so neat that God can speak to us through a bird, a donkey, a rainbow, a sign, a song—or whatever He chooses.

The eagles fly alone. They are monogamous. They stay faithful to one partner until death parts them. The eagle is an excellent example for marriages today. It would be honorable and morally sound and good for all marriages to be blessed and for no one to ever get a divorce.

I have had two husbands, and I say, "Stand by your man—because you can." I know there are situations when women cannot do this, but, when they can, it just takes effort. We have to love them no matter what they do, and then we will not depart from them until death.

I love the example of the eagles being loyal to their mates and remaining with them for life. Eagles also have the ability to see miles away from where they are. This is something that I am learning to do, to look to my future while I am still here on earth.

There will be a condition or event in my future that will launch me on my course. It will begin something new in my life, and God is already there, because He planned it for me before I was even born.

I can get excited about my future and the quality of my future that my precious God had prepared for me. By faith I have seen my future, and I believe I will fulfill my purpose.

God is a good God. He has prepared my future and keeps me for that moment. My life is already predestined by God.

I believe that I shall see the goodness of God in my life and the lives of my family.

The eagle presents a majestic picture. It's a powerful bird and it has strong, soaring wings. That's why the eagle is used as a symbol of strength.

Eagles fascinate me and inspire me. I can close my eyes and see myself soaring in the sky with wings like an eagle. I am enjoying myself in this captured moment of ecstasy.

Exodus 19:4 says, "I bore you on eagles' wings and I brought you to myself. Set you apart to be holy and worship me." I claim this Scripture for all widows. We wonder why we are left here on earth. I am realizing it's to be a worshiper of our mighty God even during the hardest part of our lives. The proof is in the pudding, because here I am, still alive.

I have survived with my God. I joyfully danced before Him, receiving peace in my heart, especially as I have been writing this book.

This does not mean that I never cried or missed Claude, because I did. I am surviving, and that is a miracle in itself.

I can live alone now, but the Lord is my strength and my personal bravery. I will not stand in terror, but I will walk and dance to make spiritual progress in my life. I want to soar above the circumstances in my life.

I am letting God be my keeper, just as the birds do. I have to keep calm and carry on with my life.

I have to dream as if I will live forever and live as if I have only today. I know the birds do this. They just fly around and take in the beauty of God's nature. They live to their fullest capacity.

I told my sister, Nancy, that our husbands were not our purpose in life. Nancy was married to Joe York, Claude's brother. Joe went to be with the Lord in the year 2001. Nancy and I are both still here on earth, but our husbands and the fathers of our children are not.

We have had to go on with our lives and use our faith. We've had to be sure of what we hope for and certain of what we do not see. We enjoyed the times when we all were together. Now, as I look back at the little things we did, I realize they were big things.

No one can take our memories from us. Nancy and I shall live on to see our husbands again in the future. What great men they both were! Our children loved them dearly. Claudanna, Claude Jr., Christi, and Jeremy are double cousins—because Claude and Joe were brothers and Nancy and I are sisters. You can tell by looking at them that our children are related to each other. I can look at our children and see their daddies' images, and I know they are as good as their daddies too.

Claude, Joe, Nancy, and I all went to a church youth camp to minister together in July 1985. All of us and our children and the children that came to the camp learned a lot about nature that summer.

I was forty years old, and I had just recorded my first record album.

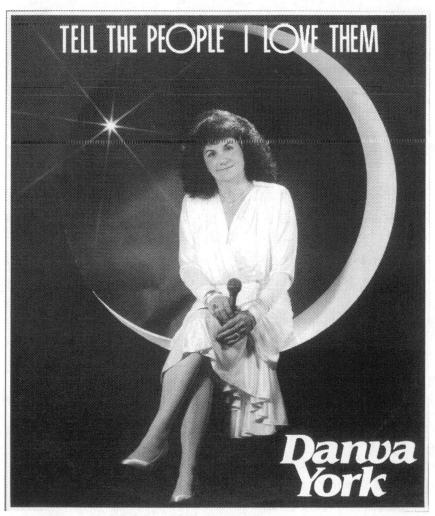

My record album "Tell The People I Love Them" and I do that for my Jesus.

I had brought some albums to give to the youth. It was titled *Tell the People I Love Them*. This was also one of the songs on my album. As I sang to the teenagers though, I changed the words of the song to "*Tell the Teenagers I Love Them*" to minister to them.

I saw snakes, scorpions, and spiders, which I could have done without seeing, but also the beauty of the birds and the flowers. They blessed me.

My memory of all of us being together that summer and working for the Lord has a special place in my heart. There were no phone calls to answer, and I liked that!

One night, I went to the boys' dorm to talk to Claude. As I left, I heard dogs barking. I ask a man who helped at the campground why the dogs were barking. He said, "Oh, they are just barking at the snakes."

I said, "Snakes! Oh my goodness let me get back to the girls' dorm!"

One day in church, I saw scorpions crawling around the top of the ceiling. I prayed they would not fall on anyone. I love nice animals like horses, cows, eagles, birds, dogs and cats. I'd rather not be out in the country with all those other kinds of wildlife. Let's face it: I don't like snakes and bugs. Ha! I love riding horses in the country though.

When I worked at Daystar Television, Josie Garcia found a beautiful picture of birds for my desktop background. I love that picture. It was so nice of Josie to find it for me. That's the kind of wildlife I enjoy seeing every day!

I know Claude and Joe are having a ball touring heaven together. I am so happy for both of them. They both deserve it.

That summer we became like the spiritual dad and mom to a lot of children at the camp. Those are memories that no one can take from us. They will always have a special place in my heart.

My mother, who was an artist, told my brother, sisters, and me that she wanted to paint a picture for us. Mother gave us the choice of what the picture would be. I chose the picture of birds that Josie had put on my computer at work. I wanted all the birds to be yellow to match my bathroom upstairs.

I call the upstairs bathroom my "sunshine room," and those birds bless me in that room. I sit by the window to sing and worship God after my bath. It is like a cleansing for me—not just for my body but also for my spirit.

The birds do remind me of Mother and her wonderful talent. I appreciate that she took the time to paint something for us that we can enjoy all of our lives. My mother went to heaven just after she had finished our pictures.

We knew Mother only had two weeks to live. Rick and Phyllis Holder, my brother-in law and my sister, let my brother, sisters, Claude, and I stay at their house. We all stayed with Mother, and we had a wonderful time together.

We knew that the day of her home-going had come. Phyllis turned to me and said, "Danva, let's sing the song 'Holy Spirit, You Are Welcome in This Place.'"

As we began to sing, we saw a different color than her normal skin tone start to come up through Mother's hands and go up her arms to the top of her body. Then it disappeared. We actually saw our mother's spirit leave her body. We know the Holy Spirit came and took her to heaven. That was such a wonderful thing to see, and it blessed us all so much!

What happened that day would be an excellent picture to capture on a canvas. I wish Mother could have painted it for us. I think the people who do not believe that God is real would have believed it that day.

I am so grateful to Rick and Phyllis for letting us stay at their house with Mother in her last days. I will never forget it.

Claude walked around their property a lot during those two weeks. He loved being outside because he was raised in the country. I can see him in my mind's eye right now, swinging in their swing and enjoying the outdoors. He was glad they had a swing like the one in the front of our house.

When Mother went to be with Jesus, Claude was outside walking. Only her children were with her. I think Mother took us all in her spiritual arms and said, "Let me cuddle my babies that I bore, in my arms, one last time." Then she went to meet her Maker.

God gives me the beginning of each day. He allows me each day to use as I choose. I can waste it or I can use it for good. What I do today is important because I am exchanging a day of my life for it.

I determined today to set aside time to work on this book. I chose not to talk on the phone, watch television, go anyplace, or do anything in my home. I have to dedicate my time to my book so I can present a book that will encourage others to understand that they can make it, even though they have lost a loved one.

After I pray, I begin to type what the Lord gives to me. You can apply this same method to anything you do in life. You have to focus on your goal, trusting God to help you and plan your way.

When tomorrow comes, this day will be gone forever, leaving in its place something I have traded for it. I want it to be gain and not loss, good and not evil, success and not failure, for the price I have paid.

I know the feeling you get in your stomach when the one you love is gone and you cannot talk to them anymore. I have had to walk it out and search with all my heart and then listen to God to lead me to find peace in the midst of the storm.

The little birds have played a big part in my confidence of moving into my future with hope. The sparrows do not worry; they're fed by Jesus, who watches over them. What is the price of five sparrows—a couple of pennies? As God's Word says in Luke 12:6–7 (TLB), God does not forget a single one of them. That passage also says that the very hairs on our heads are all numbered. I will not be afraid anymore.

When I am all alone, I think of what Mama Miller (my grandmother) told me she did every night. She had so much wisdom and faith in Jesus. I will share now her sweet words.

Mama and Papa Miller and Aunt Hattie they are my jewels in heaven.

I once asked her, "Mama Miller, since Papa went to heaven, do you get scared at night, since Papa is not here at night with you?"

She said, "Oh, no, honey! I just pray before I go to bed and say, 'It's you and me, Jesus.' Then I go right off to sleep." This is worth saying over and over, and it works.

I have started saying this at night too, before I go to bed. I thank you, Mama Miller, for sharing that with me. What a revelation of someone trusting Jesus to protect them. Just like the birds, which probably say in their bird language, "No fear lives here."

I have to trust Jesus too and live each day like there is no tomorrow. God is my husband now, and I am so glad I can lean on Him.

God hangs out the stars and He tells the sun to shine. He kisses the flowers each morning with dew. God is not too busy to make something new—to use my life for His glory, for something He planned—even before I knew what I would do.

Today, as I stood outside in front of my house, four birds started circling above me. They began to perform an air show for me, diving and going up and down. It was a beautiful sight.

It reminded me of the helicopters at the Bell Helicopter air shows. Claude would take our family, and they were exciting to see. He was so proud to work for Bell Helicopter, and he enjoyed making the parts for them.

The company gave him a very nice retirement party and presented him with gold helicopters in a gold frame for his devoted service after thirty-eight years.

I just thank Jesus for letting the birds come and minister to me and give me a touch of joy to spark hope for my day. I can see in the birds their freedom to live life with purpose. They fly without a care and perform in the sky as if they are doing acrobatic dives for all to see.

How exciting it is to see God's little creations bless me! I know they really are sent to me by God to give me joy, so that I can say, "I love it, I love it, I love it!"

Today I went into my backyard and saw a beautiful butterfly. I know God sent it to me to beautify my day and make me blissfully happy. I love to watch butterflies as they go from place to place.

I see that God is using nature more and more to help me as I go through my journey so that I can see the beauty of life. I look for laughter more than I ever have before, in just plain, ordinary places. I know the light of Jesus shines down on me. He is sending His nature to cheer my heart.

I followed the butterfly around to the side of my house, and the first thing I saw was our rose bush. I had not noticed it this past year. Claude would always bring me roses from that bush. I heard a small whisper inside me saying, "Go pick some roses." I went into the kitchen and got my scissors and proceeded to cut some roses. As I began to cut a stem, my scissors broke. I began to laugh and thought, *I didn't do this right.*

I had to get pliers to break the stem, but in the end—praise God—I got some roses off our bush. By the way, I got a few thorns in my fingers, but my tenacity got me my roses.

I realized Claude was strong enough to pick roses without pliers, but not me. I have to learn to laugh at my inability to get a rose the first try. I wish he could bring me roses again. When I get to heaven, he can.

I have read books about people who have gone to heaven, and they say there are roses.

Trying to get the roses was something, like my going on with my life. Even though I am missing Claude so much, I intend to persevere in my life to find what God still has for me to do. I took my roses and took possession of them. Then I went and sat in Claude's swing for the first time in nearly a year.

As a teenager, I used to climb mountains and with my best friend, Sharie McAlister, in Indiahoma, Oklahoma.

Sharie and Danva we will be best friends forever, she and I always have fun.

As we climbed the mountains, we could hear their sweet music, and as we neared the top it seemed to be louder and sweeter. We could also hear our echoes and the echoing of nature.

Sharie and I also rode horses on her dad's farm in the pastures; the wind would speak to me. The horses would move with a long swinging gallop, as the wind spoke to me, "Enjoy." We rode on the horses with no saddles; in the creek bed and it was wild and fun. The rocks and leaves would make a sound, as our horses were loping with the hoofs on their feet. The sound of freedom was in the air as nature sang its own song.

Nature's peace flowed through me as I held the roses. It was the same feeling as reaching the top of the mountains. Just as the sunshine flowed at the top of the mountain and in the rose bush, the wind blew freshness into me. I felt my cares drop away.

I held my roses and, in my heart, it seemed as if Claude had come down and given them to me.

Day and night alike belong to our God. He made the starlight and the sun. All nature is within His hands. He made the winter and summer too.

I want to always find the beauty in nature as I go through the rest of my life. I want to carry that beauty with me in my heart, so that I can impart it to others.

We all will experience new chapters in our life. We have to adjust to them. I have had to confront and adapt to the changes in my life because they were things that I could not ignore. I have become independent for the first time in my life, and I am so glad God gave me His Son Jesus as my guide.

My emotions have been up and down. Some people have seen me as I worked through them. Life without emotions would be easier, but it would be colorless and unexciting.

I know God made tears, and after I have let my emotions spill forth I just have a good cry and then I am all better.

I am not talking about a depressing spirit trying to attack. I am talking about releasing the joy that God puts in us. This comes from the refreshment of the washing of tears from our eyes.

God made us humans, not robots. As I look at nature, it speaks to me to carry on, to become an eagle in my life, in whatever task that has been set before me by my heavenly Father. I have to run the race set before me and continue on.

Sometimes, I feel alone, but I am never alone. Jesus said, "I will never leave you nor forsake you." I think that is enough for me. How about you?

There is only one person or thing that can defeat me in this life, and that is myself. And I do not intend to do that. I am more than a conqueror through Jesus Christ.

Chapter Nine

DANCE, DAN DEE, DANCE!

I AM DAN DEE AND I AM ready to dance for Jesus in my Texas outfit.

My sweet Daddy nicknamed me Dan Dee, and that is the reason I have titled this chapter "Dance, Dan Dee, Dance!" My daddy would pick me up and dance around with me when I was smaller. He taught me about living my life to be happy, having a good sense of humor, and living for Jesus.

God has set my feet to dancing, and He wants me to share with you about it. Psalm 149:3 (NIV) says, "Let them praise his name with dancing." Ecclesiastes 3:4 says, "There is a time to dance."

It is the time for me to dance now more than ever before. I have been through some ups and downs these past nine months. I have had to literally dance to keep myself above my circumstances. God has turned my mourning into dancing. What a joy to know the pleasure of dancing before the Lord and to dance to good, clean music to lift my spirit to joy! I have always danced and worshiped my God.

Claude and I would dance together at church, and many people told us how much it blessed them to see us in unity. We even danced to Jewish music around both of my daughters and their husbands at their wedding receptions. Jesus has done so much for my family and me. I want to show Him I can dance before Him, to honor Him.

David in the Bible wanted to honor God. To honor Him and worship Him in the dance does bring me joy!

The highest calling we have is to be worshipers of our mighty God. I earnestly want to do important, serious business for my God.

God let Jesus, His son, die so that I may have life and have it more abundantly. I want to express the truth of how I made it through the hard times, especially when the tears and loneliness came.

As I dance, I believe God dances with me. Claude bought me a Precious Moments plaque in the shape of a heart, and it says, "God danced the day you were born. You are loved. You are beautiful. You are a gift of God."

This plaque Claude gave me will cause me to dance forever. It is because I do know God dances. He created the dance for us to express our worship and love for Him. I want to be a graceful, gracious, grateful woman for God.

Barbara Pendleton at Calvary Cathedral Church told me she saw a vision in which angels were lifting my feet up as I danced before the Lord. She gave me the Scripture Malachi 4:2 (TLB): "You will go free, leaping with joy." She said, "Danva, you have always worshipfully danced before

God. From now on, you will go forth and jump about playfully to be released, to leap for joy!"

Wow! She was prophesying, fifteen years ago, what I am doing now. I have done this many times whenever I start missing Claude. All through my life, God has done great and marvelous things. He has ordered my steps to dance, and I am so happy to do that for my wonderful God!

Knowing the angels had a part in my dancing makes me feel very honored, to be able to dance for my King Jesus and have heaven's hand on me.

One day, on March 12, 1980, at Calvary Cathedral Church, I was worshipping God and dancing before Him. I had my mind on God and how much I loved Him when all of a sudden many children surrounded me. They said to me, "We are from the Texas Pythian Children's Home in Weatherford, Texas. It has given us joy to see you dancing in church."

A lady from Texas Pythian Home had brought them to church. I know she will have rewards in heaven waiting for her. The children said, "We have never seen someone dance in church. Will you come see us at the Pythian home to visit us?"

And I said, "Yes, I will come."

I asked my friend Linda Barnett Dolney, who lived in Weatherford, to go with me. We were friends and had gone to Calvary together for years.

Claude, Linda, and I went to the Pythian Home, and we were so blessed to minister to those children. I could see the hand of God on the dance then and now to uplift children and adults, to bring them joy and the hope that life can be fun.

We continued to visit those children, and every time we were so blessed. We fell in love with those children, and they loved us in return.

Remembering how we reached out to those children years ago, I decided to include that story in my book. It's exciting! The experience of meeting them was all because I was dancing before the Lord.

How amazing God is! He knew they would be acknowledged, years later. He knew the dance would begin a wonderful relationship with God's little orphan angels.

There came a time when I had to have foot surgery. Most of my sisters had to have the same surgery. I call this a curse manifested, but, since then, I have broken that curse off us.

We were going to Calvary to church, but Claude wanted us to go to Kenneth Copeland's church so I would not have to climb all the stairs at Calvary. At Kenneth Copeland's church, I was able to elevate my feet on a board they had attached to the chairs in front of me. This kept my foot from swelling.

I became very protective of my feet. I didn't want anyone to step on them!

Needless to say, the enemy did try to stop me from dancing. The bones in my feet were tender from the surgery, and I had to wait for them to heal properly before I could dance again.

I did use wisdom and I did not dance for a while. When I was able to dance again, I said, "I have missed my time in worship to you, God. I take my authority over you, Devil, and I am going to dance! This is my time with God, and I know He will dance with me."

Just remember there is light at the end of the tunnel. Whatever you face in life, there is an answer to your need. God has laid out the path we have to walk. The enemy must flee when we resist him.

When I took that first step after surgery, I could feel pain, but I had to resist it and, by faith, dance for my King Jesus. What a victory for my future! If I had let fear enter me, I would never have danced again. I would not have that outlet to release the joy God gives to me in dance. Now when I dance because I miss Claude, I know dancing will release joy in me.

I have always prayed the Word of God over my family, my friends, myself, and prayer requests given to me. I began to compile Scriptures for my feet. Now I see God's plan in that. I didn't know I would write a book and share my journey with you—to show you how God has used my feet for His glory.

Dr. Barney Stumbo from Calvary Cathedral gave me this Scripture (Isaiah 52:7) for my feet and prayed it over me: "How beautiful upon the mountains are the feet of him who brings good tidings, who publishes peace, who brings good tidings of good, who publishes salvation."

I believe God was saying through this Scripture to me, "You are a soul winner." I am an evangelist at heart and I love to lead people to Jesus, so this is true.

People have told me my feet are attractive. Recently, I was in an elevator and a lady looked down at my feet and said, "You have beautiful feet."

I said, "Thank you, and to God be the glory."

I am not trying to brag about my feet. I am just sharing that your feet can be anointed. I want God to get the glory. I never take that compliment as being about myself but about the Jesus in me. I believe this means for me to be a soul winner.

I have a date written down in my Bible near Isaiah 52:7. It was on September 29, 1996, that Dr. Stumbo prayed that verse over me. God gave me feet to dance before him in worship.

I want to share these Scriptures with you and tell you that I confessed and I claimed them until the healing manifested in my feet. I made all the Scripture personal for me. This is how I prayed the Word of God over me. This is my way of confessing the Word, but not direct quotes from the Word.

1 Samuel 2:9: "God, thank you for guarding my feet as I walk and dance."

2 Samuel 22:34: "God, you make my feet like the hind's feet, firm and stable to walk and dance."

2 Samuel 22:37: "God, you have enlarged my steps under me and my feet will not slip."

Nehemiah 9:21: "I trust you, God; to sustain me and my feet will not swell."

Psalm 18:26: "Thank you, my Lord, for plenty of room for my steps under me to walk, to dance, and my feet do not slip."

Psalm 26:12: "My feet will stand on an even place; in the congregations, I will bless my God in the dance."

Psalm 40:2: "God sets my feet upon a rock, steadying my steps as I walk and dance."

Psalm 56:13: "My God has kept my feet from falling. Now I can walk and dance before God in the light of life and the living."

Proverbs 31:17–18: "I do gird myself with strength for my physical fitness to dance, for my God-given task. I taste and see my gain from work, for God is good.

Ephesians 6:15: "I shod my feet for preparation to face the enemy with a firm-footed stability, produced by the gospel of peace."

Hebrews 12:13: "I make firm, smooth, straight paths for my feet for walking and dancing. I will make happy paths and I will go in the right direction for my life."

Some people have called me for prayer and told me they were depressed and sad. I tell them to dance and their sadness will leave them. I tell them that Psalm 150:4 says, "To praise God in the dance."

I think that if more people would dance, they would feel so much better and even keep their weight down. I think dancing is good for your heart and is an excellent exercise. The uplifting of your spirit and the joy that you receive are also a workout for your body.

The flow as you dance is like the rising of the tide in the ocean. The effort I make lets my Creator know that I will unashamedly dance before Him and bring Him the honor that He deserves.

I always dance as if no one is watching except God. I turn off thinking about anyone but my King.

Some people say to me, "I can't dance because I don't have rhythm."

I tell them, "Listen to the beat of the music; step out by faith, and the rhythm will come." Do not wait for circumstances to be favorable to dance. Begin by faith to worship God.

The rhythm is on the inside of you. He has planted it there and it will be expressed as you begin to dance. Dancing is a provision to put a person into a position to receive joy from God and to let grief go. Even if you can only move your body back and forth while sitting in a chair, you are letting God know you are worshiping him.

I want to describe to you the art of creativity as I dance and how I let my feet form, the beauty of fulfilling my feelings about God. God planned for me to write this book even before I was in my mother's womb. He moved upon my heart to share my experiences with others.

God wants to see a demonstration from His people, which will show our love for Him. He takes pleasure when we dance before Him.

I have always loved to dance, and I have danced some places where I shouldn't have. Claude and I were at a dance place, and while we were dancing I said to myself, "What if Jesus should come back while I am dancing with Claude to honky-tonk music? I know we are in a beer joint (even though we are not drinking). I also know Jesus would be very displeased with us."

God began to speak to my heart. I was to have no part with unfruitful works of darkness, as in Ephesians 5:11, and I was to abstain from all appearance of evil, as in 1 Thessalonians 5:22 (KJV). I never went back to one of those places again.

Dancing is not wrong. It depends on where you are, the kind of music, and who you are dancing for. At that time in my life, my church did not allow dancing in church. I knew there was dancing to be released in me.

Needless to say, I had a lesson to learn, as I always have in my life. Praise God, I am to be an over comer. I am still learning about life every day. I always say, "Remind me, Lord that I am human, and human beings forget. Help me to be like you and let my life reflect your image. Show me what you brought me from and where I could have been."

God kept me from going to a burning hell when he allowed me to let my dance be for Him. He supplied me with a church where I could worship God in dance.

It was all in God's plan for me to dance, and now I encourage others to do the same. When I begin to feel grief, I go to the room that I have made for myself to dance. I begin to dance, and of course no one is watching except God.

My life isn't about how I survived the storm of losing my two husbands; it is about how I danced while going through the storm. I have danced more since Claude's going to heaven than I ever danced before. I have made it because dancing releases the joy of the Lord in my soul!

There are fun, clean dances too, and it's the Golden Oldies music. It gives me a good workout and a lot of memories of my teenage years, and it's good, clean fun.

I have gone to sing at the nursing homes for about twenty-three years now. I recorded my first record album because I enjoyed singing for the senior citizens, which gives them pleasure. It has only been lately that I have started taking the Golden Oldies music to the nursing homes.

My granddaughter, Bethany, downloaded this music for me. I started dancing to it in my home, and I felt such delight. I have such fun with those songs. When I take music to the nursing homes, I give them the name of the songs I have and I let them pick out the music that brought them pleasure when they were younger. You should see their happy faces! If they can't get up and dance, I have them tap their feet or clap their hands. It is such a blessing to see them happy!

I can now see the reasons God put the desire to dance in my heart, and they are all the reasons I have mentioned. I can say that the Spirit of the Lord is upon the dance, for worship or for fun! God has placed things on this earth for us to enjoy, but not misuse.

I think God has a sense of humor and He likes for us to have one too—so go for it! We should show the world we can have good, clean fun and have the joy of the Lord too.

I used to work for Daystar Television where Marcus and Joni Lamb are the founders. Working for them was an enjoyable time in my life. I retired to be with Claude after he retired. I decided to visit Daystar the other day, to see all my friends there. It was such a blessing to see them.

Many of them reminded me that, when I worked there, I always danced at our worship time. They said they would never forget how I worshiped God. I am so glad that I could leave them with a good memory. I had not thought about that in a while. It makes me so happy that I can share my memories in this book. We never know how people are watching our lives. A simple thing like worshiping God in dance can influence people for the good.

On February 4, 2010, Prophet David Gardiner spoke over me. He said God was going to cause tremendous joy and happiness to flood my soul and my feet would start dancing. The Lord was going to put a new melody in my heart and a new a song within me. He was going to give me peace in the midst of the storm. God did that just for me.

Even when there was a part of me that didn't feel like rejoicing or dancing, the Lord has restored the joy of my salvation. The Lord has caused my heart to be able to laugh and rejoice. He saw me praying over the young and the adults alike, and He has turned my mourning into dancing. The anointing of joy has come upon me and my feet will go to dancing. That prophecy has come to pass.

At Gospel Way Church on January 16, 2011, I ministered to the youth and adults, and then we worshipped God in the dance together. It was awesome, and I was so blessed.

I do appreciate another word from Prophet David Gardiner, which I received on August 27, 2010. He said, "Danva, I see over your life joy, love, and excitement in you. This will be a rejoicing time. The Lord will cause your spirit man to come alive inside by worshipping and praising Him."

He also said, "It will affect your whole health and the anointing will be touching you, your spirit, your soul and body. The Lord will literally renew your strength and put new life and healing touches inside you. You will be able to run and leap over a wall in the spirit. In the days to come, you will be able to comfort others that are going through the valley you have. You will help many people who are at their wit's end. You will encourage them, bless them, and share your testimonies. You will share how the Lord helped you, how He is your comforter, and how He is showing you things."

I received this Word, and this is already happening. On September 11, 2010, I went to a ladies meeting at Word of Love Christian Center. Pastor Shirlene Moore and invited me to come I was glad she did. During the worship, the worship leader asked us to come to the altar and worship God in the dance. Since it was not my church, I hesitated going down. I decided to go and just be free to dance there too.

After the worship, a lady came up to me and said she saw a vision of me dancing and I was a little girl. She said, "Our Father God was so pleased with your dancing. He wants more of His children to become more childlike." This is what Prophet David had spoken over me, which was another confirmation.

I am beginning to see so many different things happening in my life. It is so exciting to let God order my steps and just have plain old fun and stay above my circumstances.

My life is about fulfilling the destiny that I could not have planned if I had wanted to. God is God, and He does not want anyone else to take His job. He is quite capable of ordering my steps and your steps. If we take a detour, guess what? God will get us back on the right road.

I always tell people to use the traffic signals as an example to tell you if you are driving on the right road. If the traffic light is red, that means stop where you are. If the traffic light is yellow, that means to use caution in where you are going. If the traffic light is green, then go ahead. It is all in the plan of God for us to discern and give us the peace of God. If you do not have peace, don't do whatever you were planning. Peace is the green light and our guidance from God.

I want to share with you the following song I wrote on December, 24, 2000: It is titled "Blessed Is My Body."

Blessed are my feet I dance and walk on.
Blessed are my legs that hold me up.
Blessed are my knees that do not buckle.
I am redeemed and I am strong.
Blessed are my hands that lay hands on others.
Blessed are my eyes that see my eyes healed.
Blessed is my heart that gives love to others.
As I seed into them, I am healed.
Jesus came to redeem me.
The curse is reversed because of the cross.
Now I have restoration.
My life begins and never ends.
Only because of the blood of Jesus he shed for me.
Jesus is my best friend and He loves even me.
I can dance and I am set free.

Let go and let God set your feet to dancing, if He has not already done that for you. Be blessed by using your own feet and legs.

There is a song we sing in church that says, "Dance, children, dance, and I will set you free." Life is a song, and love is the dance and music. There are those who say only sunshine brings happiness, but they have never danced in the rain. I will be happy and dance merrily, for in Jeremiah 31:4 (KJV) the Word of God says I can.

Joy will replace mourning. I am taking that to my heart, and I am applying it to my life.

I say, Dance Dan Dee Dance and my Daddy in heaven is cheering me on.

Chapter Ten

HOLD ONTO GOD

I SAY: HOLD ONTO GOD NO MATTER what happens or how discouraging your situation may become. I will never stop clinging to my God. He is so trustworthy, and I know I can run to Him and I can talk to Him.

I have asked God, "Why did you leave me here by myself? Do you think I am tough or what?"

I believe God knows our emotions and our thoughts, and He does not become upset if we ask a question of Him. I knew the answer to my own question, but I guess I thought that I could get more insight into His will by asking him for clarification.

I know I have not finished my assignment here on earth yet. God has specific purposes for me to fulfill for Him. I know that writing this book is one of these purposes.

As I am looking at my life today, I am letting go of what has been and learning to speak in a new way. I want to have my own unique style of expressing myself—not only in my book but also in my life.

I am allowing God to show me new possibilities with many opportunities to be creative, and I am giving God all the glory. As I learn God's will, I can see starlight after the storm. I have satisfaction in my life and live every moment with new expectations.

I must make the most of my opportunities to tell others about Jesus. I have to make it plain and be bold enough to tell it freely and fully. This has been a time for me to seek God more than I ever have before in my life, according to Hosea 10:12 (AMP). He rains His righteous gift of salvation on me. He desires for me to share with others what He has done in my life.

It is not an easy thing to be widowed twice and still believe there is a purpose for you.

But I am going to believe that my vision will be bigger than what it is today, and it will come to pass. I believe that I am endowed with courage. I know God will qualify me and perfect the places in my life that need to be.

God has created in me a clean heart and has renewed a right spirit within me, because I am depending on Him. I do repent every time I know that I have missed the mark and also every night before I go to bed, because I know I do not have a promise of tomorrow. I do not want to have anything standing between my God and me.

It takes a lot of pressure off me, knowing God is in control of my life. Sometimes, I know I get *spankings* from Him, but He is only bringing me to a place of continually holding fast to His love and mercy.

Working my way through my journey and holding onto God's unchanging hand is the most elating thing I can do, to raise my spirit as I go to the next level of the acceptance of any situation I face.

I try to do activities to set a pace to steer my emotions in a positive direction. Sometimes, things do bring tears, but tears are the body's release valve for the emotions of grief. If I kept all the grief inside me, it would be physically destructive. I learned years ago to let it out and not keep all my emotions inside.

God made tears as one of His healing balms. It releases a peace inside me. I am not talking about a continuous flow of tears that never stops— that would be a spirit of grief trying to attach itself to me. I am talking about a refreshing and a cleansing. As an example, it's like when I wash my clothes and they come out smelling fresh and clean.

Normal tears are a washing away of sadness that leads to gladness. I pray this statement will put a sparkle in your eye and a kick in your step.

Believe me: I have walked through some tough times. I have cried, but turning to God's unchanging hand was my key to open the door for joy. I have found renewed energy in creating a new life for myself.

In spite of all of my emotions, God has encircled me with His grace and mercy and has never given up on me. I have learned to encounter the abundant presence of God, to receive His touch and hold onto Him.

God, who began a good work in me, will see me through my journey to my destination. He has never given up on me, and I am so grateful that He hasn't.

According to Proverbs 25:11, "A word fitly spoken in due season is like apples of gold in settings of silver." I hope my voice speaks to you as you read my book.

I want to give encouragement to the brokenhearted and release a blessing to them. I titled the music CD that I recorded *A Silver Setting* because Jesus is my precious silver treasure. He died for all of us on the cross, which was a catastrophic plot of Satan.

Jesus died for us, but He rose again from the grave and proved He was king. He did that so we would have life and have it abundantly. He is the gate for us to walk through in life.

The challenge of rebuilding my life has been based on a guideline for my life, which is the Word of God. I acknowledge that my life has been forever changed and I am willing to see what is yet to come. I have been able to laugh and see the sun shining brightly again.

As I have walked through this last year, I wrote this chorus to my Jesus: "I Thank You, Lord."

I want to thank You, Lord, and I say *Danke schoen* (thank you), as the Germans say.

I want to thank You, Lord, and I say *Ich liebe dich* (I Love You), as the Germans say.

I want to thank You, Lord, for letting me soar to heights like the eagles do, so I can know You more.

I want to thank You, Lord, for letting me reign as a king and sing like a queen.

I want to thank You, Lord, for making me healthy and strong and giving me a new song.

I want to thank You, Lord, for making me whole and saving my soul.

I want to thank You, Lord, for helping me to be in one accord and for being my husband and my Lord.

I want to thank You, Lord, for helping me to be cheerful and not fearful.

I want to thank You, Lord, for giving me my good friends and I want to be a good friend.

I want to thank You, Lord, for giving me my life now; in reverence to you I bow.

Jesus, Danke schoen! Jesus, Ich liebe dich!"

God has already thought out the things that have come into my life and knows His purpose for them. I believe my wilderness experience has been a launching pad for my destiny.

I may not be living on the mountain, but I refuse to live in the valley. I choose to live right in the middle, climb that mountain, and be a mountain mover. I have determined to reach for God's best, and I have made the decision to receive all that God has for me.

My words are seeds that start the process for my future. I have a choice: I can live by the Word of God or I can choose to live by circumstances. I have decided to live by the Word of God, to decree it in my life. I believe the Word will produce my thinking, and my thinking produces my decisions. My right decisions will produce happiness.

I am going to hold onto God and receive His blessings. God is a good God, and I want to follow His leading with all my heart. I want to make a resolution to walk in love, live by faith, make specific decisions to believe, and receive all that God has for me. I have to hear by the Spirit of God, not just God's words, but hear the sound of His voice. I have to hold onto God. I do not see how people make it in life if they don't hold onto God.

James Cash Penney, who later built the J. C. Penney stores, had a wilderness experience. He lost forty million dollars in the stock market crash of 1929 and became deathly ill from the stress of the loss. He wrote farewell letters to his family because he wanted to die. He waited for the end. He felt he was a failure at the age of fifty-six.

Mr. Penney felt he had no future, but God had other plans. At a sanitarium where Penney was being treated for his illness, he heard the hymn "God Will Take Care of You," and he decided to trust Jesus as his Savior. He did survive. He lived into his nineties and built a financial empire through his J. C. Penney stores. Mr. Penney is an example for all of us.

We can hold onto God no matter what we face. As I hold onto God, I expect to be an overcomer. Without a mountain, I couldn't be a very good overcomer.

I will do the things He has called me to do. I declare that I will see God turn the things I have gone through around for my good. I have seen many miraculous manifestations of His power in my life, and I know I will see more.

I am going to live in a state of expectancy of God's supernatural manifestations in every day of my life. I want to live in such a way that I can please Him in everything I do.

I have to live by faith, and as I partake of faith it is as natural as breathing. If I had to somehow work up my faith, I would not make it, and I would not be victorious. Faith is for my benefit in whatever I need, and it means having confidence, belief, and trust in God. "Faith does come by hearing, and hearing by the word of God" (Romans 10:17 KJV).

As I walk through my house and I am alone, I embrace the memories of the years

I have lived here. I remember wonderful occasions: Christmas, Thanksgiving, Bible studies, prayer meetings, parties, wedding showers, baby showers, and birthdays. We were all like an angel with one wing, and we could only fly by embracing each other.

For such a time as this, I am here alone and have no one to embrace, but no one can take away my memories. We made so many friends through the years, and now I am making new friends and new memories. It is helping to make a difference in my life.

I cannot live in the past—I can only remember it. I now live for today and I take it only one day at a time. My hope for my future is to hold onto God. He is faithful, and it is comforting to know He will be there for me.

I have purposed in my heart to hear God's voice. I am doing a simple thing by quieting myself down so that I can fix my eyes on God. To recognize His voice as spontaneous thoughts, that did appear as a light in my mind. In writing this book, I have had to hold onto God like never before. To hear God's voice is so very important to me, because I don't have Claude to balance me out anymore.

I have to deepen my knowledge of God's Word so I can be the person He wants me to be.

By faith, I see my future. My desire is for God to take me places where I cannot ask to be taken, because I don't even know they exist.

I love to laugh, have fun, experience new things, and enjoy life. I am still here on earth, so God is not through with me. My life is not over, so I will continue to live life to the fullest.

I want to be at the right place at the right time and experience adventures in new places. I want to be with people to share the good news with them. I want to hear God's voice telling me where to go every day of my life.

I have learned I can hear God for myself. I have to rely on Him and not other people, because he already has a plan for me anyway, according to Psalm 25:4–5.

I can ask God to show me His ways, to teach me His paths, and to guide me in His truth. I know God wants us to be prepared people and to win others to Jesus. He sends people across our paths. He did this with me when He sent my daughter, Anju, all the way from India to America and me. God allowed me the honor to lead Anju to Jesus. My desire is to lead others to Jesus.

When I yield to Him, He begins to do something new. Instead of always reaching out for the familiar, I want to reach out for the unknown. Sometimes, we are the Bible to people who do not go to church or read their Bibles. We, as Christians, have to show people that we are representatives of Jesus.

I love going to the ocean and watching the waves and hearing the roaring of the sea. God formed the great springs in the depths of the oceans. He set the limits of the seas and gave them instructions not to spread beyond their boundaries.

The mighty oceans thunder their praise to God. The Lord on high is mightier and more glorious than the noise of many waters and mightier than the storms and the waves of the sea.

When I recount His illustrious acts, I recall how, in the heat of the battle that I faced, He was like the calmness of the sea after a storm.

He gave me strength and many songs—songs of joy that came to my rescue as I sang them in my home. I thought I would not make it without Claude, but I did not die.

I am living to tell you the strong arm of the Lord has done glorious things for me. I am living to write this book and tell of His deeds.

God has given me His peace like a gentle river and great waves of righteousness. It is like they came together; kissed each other, and mercy and loving kindness came to me.

He has blessed me with my children and grandchildren who have been to me like the offspring of the sea. They are a part of their dad and papa that I can still see. I cherish the memories of us going on vacations to the ocean and having so much fun.

Claude would go way out into the ocean, then he would dive deep to find me seashells. I still have them. I can hold them up to my ear and imagine the sound of the ocean in them.

The sound of many waters will always bring me the gold nuggets of memories of our times at the ocean.

I can easily hold onto God. He has blessed me so much and I am very grateful. I think about the presence of God with me when I am alone, and then I say, "I am not alone! God is with me." I am immediately filled with joy at that thought. I do not want to forget that He will never leave me or forsake me. God wants to demonstrate through me that you can make it through difficult times. He wants us to become living examples to others, so they can apply His wisdom to their lives.

I have a pathway to walk. It is a step-by-step obedience to God. I chose to follow the path He has laid out for me, and I know God will grant to me the abundance of His blessings.

Sometimes, I don't know the next step down my pathway. Then I have to tell God, "I don't know where my pathway is going to be, but I step into your pathway. I know you have the best ahead for me."

When I am in the presence of God, I try to resist the temptation to think about my plans for tomorrow, next week, or next year. I have to live in that eternal moment in God. It's much better for me to relax, hold onto

God, and let Him be my guide. He knows how to drop thoughts into my spirit, and those thoughts are revelations to me.

I look at my life and all the things I have done and all the things I have. I can say I am a very blessed woman. I do not take anything for granted that I have been able to do in my life, or anything I have.

As I sit here tonight typing, I can recall many things God has taught me. I know I am to share these thoughts with others. The simplicity of God's way to do things opens the doors in your life for better things. He allows people to cross your path and bless your life. The people God has let cross my path have not been a coincidence.

Vernon and Patty my wonderful neighbors that I love dearly.

My neighbors, Vernon and Patty, are an example. God placed me right next door to them, knowing I would be here alone and I would feel safer with them. Patty is helping me again to proofread my book. What a blessing she is to me!

Howard has done so many things for me and around my house that I told him, "If I could clone you, I would." God uses people to bless us on this earth. I cannot express enough the gratitude I have for everyone who has reached out to me.

When I hold onto God and He sends people to me, they are like angels sent to me. How can I say thanks often enough? I want the rhythm of my footsteps to echo, "Danke schoen, danke schoen, thank you, thank you" to Vernon, Patty, Howard, and everyone who has done something for me.

I want to be the person God intends for me to be and not go off and do my own thing. I will follow peace to the destination God has for me.

It is really exciting to wait for God's plans for me to develop in my life, and I will respect them. It is like drinking organic coffee compared to regular coffee. There is a big difference to me—the organic coffee tastes much better and I enjoy it much more.

It is a lot easier for me to let God give me the desire to enjoy His plan for me.

My plans will not compare to God's plan. That is exciting to me, because I don't have to worry about the outcome.

God has already made His plan, and He is the writer of my life. I can trust in the arms of my God and just hold onto Him, and then I can go through my life peacefully, joyfully, thankfully, and victoriously.

God, I want to tell everyone how you have helped me, even from my earliest childhood. I want to constantly testify to others about the wonderful things you do for me and what others have done for me too.

Your power and goodness, Lord, reach to the highest heavens. You have made everything beautiful in its time.

God, you have demonstrated your awesome power in my life. You care about my family and me because you sent your son Jesus to pay for our sins gives me proof.

You have helped my family and I make it through this last year, with all our tears. Your goodness is seen in my life and my children's lives. I know that generations to come in my family will never forget your promises and covenant to us. You stood by us.

Your loving kindness is everlasting and you are God without beginning or end. God, you have been the foundation under my feet and have shown me where to place my next step. Your everlasting arms have been my support in conforming me to your image during my time of growing stronger in you. You have transformed me by your grace.

I will hold onto You, God, for the rest of my time here on earth. I know, God, You have so much waiting for me in heaven, but You also have a purpose for me on earth.

As I wait in hope for that glorious day, I must live by faith, knowing your hands are extended to me. Your glory will be reflected on me and your love will be expressed through me as I am fulfilling my destiny.

God is the source of my strength in every circumstance of my life. I do believe He is in control of my life and He is bringing me to my place in life, where I can live in Christ.

I want this chapter to release the best in people to hold onto God more than they ever have. We can hold on like a bulldog and let the best of us come forth in our lives.

We are in God's hands, and He wants to chart the course in our lives. As we focus on Jesus, He becomes to us all there is and all that really matters.

If there was not another human on earth except me, I would still need to focus on Jesus instead of myself and let Him be Lord of my life.

The strength and happiness for me is to find out the way God is going and go in that direction too.

Happiness is not finding a person to make you happy—it is first finding Jesus and letting Him make you happy. Other people can make you happy, but true happiness is asking Jesus to come into your heart and making Him Lord of your life.

Holding onto God is the only way I made it as I went through the loss of two husbands in my life.

Chapter Eleven

REFLECTIONS ON TWO-STORY HOUSES

I THINK THERE IS SOMETHING VERY SIGNIFICANT, momentous, and important as I share my reflections about living in two-story houses. They all have brought me to the place in my life that I am in right now.

I can say there has been a healing for me in my home. I have the walls to intensify my feelings and the rooms to encourage me to write, because there are so many memories. I encourage everyone to take the moments you had with your loved ones and put them into writing for future generations to read.

Each of the homes I shared—with my parents, brother, sisters and I; Eddie, Angela and I; Claude, Angela, Claudanna, Claude Jr. and I—has left me with inspiration. The influence of our love motivated me to write this chapter. It has helped me to carry on and stay in my home.

We enjoyed life. Even though we were not perfect, we persevered and we let our homes be a big part of our lives.

In my lifetime, I have lived in three two-story houses, and there is a story about each one. I enjoy the reflections I have about them. Living in these houses was like having two-piece dwellings. You can do a lot with that space.

I want to share my experiences in those wonderful houses. I know God planned my life to be enjoyed within the walls of these homes, including family times, Bible studies, prayer times, love, joy, peace, excitement, memories, remodeling, decorating, parties, showers, and holidays.

What cherished memories I have of my time in each one of them! There have been many intervals when my mind goes back to those moments. I often think of my charming, embellished, adorable, beautiful homes. I have been blessed to live in them and share those times with my family.

There is a quality and character in a house that distinguishes a family symbolically. It has a solid substance, which is the essential purpose for houses. Their unique qualities made them what they were to all of us.

It is like having a *kairos* moment when life reaches an appointed time for a certain family to live in a house. It is a time that God has allowed us to share our lives in that particular house.

Houses can represent your life, and the different rooms have different settings. The decor of each room contributes to what goes on in that special room.

I have always loved to decorate my homes. I have a created setting for my writing where I have everything that I need at my fingertips. It makes writing so much more enjoyable for me.

Being organized is one of my motivational gifts, and that makes me a happy camper.

The two-story home I live in now has given me the atmosphere I need to do my writing. I feel so much peace, creativity, inspiration, enthusiasm, zeal, and creating a warmth of emotion so that I can begin to write.

When Claude and I decided to pay our house off early, we claimed the Scripture in Psalm 118:5: "We called upon the Lord He answered us and set us free and in a large place." We claimed that for our large house, and it happened!

God allowed Claude to leave me with a debt-free home. He gave Claude and me the wisdom to triple up on our house payments and pay it off.

When we went to the Colonial Savings Mortgage Company to pay off the mortgage, its employees gave each of us a crystal cup with a house on it and the words, "Congratulations, free and clear." That was a time of celebration and excitement, and we did celebrate.

I told Claude, "God honored our believing His Word and set us debt-free." Claude replied, "God sure did! Let's go out to eat and celebrate!"

Claude and I are smiling because we are debt free!

We happily went to our favorite place to eat: the Mexican Inn. "Being debt free has caused a great peace to come over me," I told Claude, "I never want to go into debt again."Claude replied, "I agree with that. The same peace came over me too."

There is a special place in my heart about the word *trinity* and the number three. A trinity means a set of three. The union of the Father God, Jesus, and the Holy Spirit—the Trinity of the Godhead—has been a part of my life since I was a child. That trinity has infiltrated me with love, direction, correction, peace, joy, and protection. I will share later how the Trinity led us to the house I live in now.

The number three means a lot to me. I was the third child my parents had, I married Claude on the third day of September, and I have had three birth children. Claude and I made three payments a month until our house was paid for. I have had three red cars. I sang in a trio with my sisters, Sherry and Barbara Ann. And I have lived in three two-story houses. Now my street number ends in three. We were the third owners of our house.

I like the Scripture according to Ecclesiastes 4:12: "A threefold cord is not easily broken." These things remind me of that Scripture. The number three also reminds me of love, unity, and peace.

My first two-story house was the one I lived in with my parents and sisters in Cleburne, Texas. It was an embellished Queen Anne-style home built in or around the year 1896. I thought it was one of Cleburne's grandest older homes. I loved the porch that wrapped around the front and side of our house.

There was a screened-in porch on the upstairs of the house too, where my sisters and I loved to play. There was a great view from that porch. We enjoyed being high up so we could see the neighborhood. Outside the door to the kitchen was another screened-in porch, which opened up to a backyard with big beautiful trees.

There were huge rooms upstairs and downstairs: a parlor, living room, dining, bedroom, kitchen, and kitchenette. As you entered the house, it had a large entry hall with a beautiful staircase that wound upstairs to the three bedrooms and outside to the screened-in porch. There was gorgeous paneling all throughout the house as well as huge doors and windows; some were stained glass.

I will always remember that house. I loved it and I still do. It was a dream house to all of us.

Claudanna, my daughter, gave me a gift one Christmas: a painting of a two-story house. The painting was titled "Reflections." I was amazed at how much it looked like the two-story house I had lived in with my parents as a child.

Claudanna worked at a school, and when it had an auction she invited me to come. She said, "Mom, pick something you want and I will bid on it for you and give it to you for your Christmas present."

I said, "I like that idea, and thank you very much."

I love this painting. It still graces a wall in my home. This is why I titled this chapter "Reflections on Two-Story Houses."

I remember our dad having Bible studies and playing games with us. Mother was always cooking and sewing for us. She was an excellent cook and seamstress.

I can hear Daddy calling us, as I listen to the past. "Girls, come on into the parlor! We are going to have our Bible study and pray." I remember us girls saying, "Daddy, what book of the Bible are you going to read to us tonight? He would always make it exciting as he read to us. His personality would make it so interesting, and he even acted out some parts.

We used to run all around our big house. It was a great place to play hide-and-seek. It was every little girl's dream of a home.

Mother would make us yummy cakes, cookies, and pies. I can hear her calling in the distant past. I remember her sweet voice saying, "Girls, come and eat what your mother has baked for you." It was so very good and yummy to our tummies. We would quit our hide-and-seek game and run to the kitchen.

Upstairs, in the middle bedroom closet, I had an adventure. There was another closet behind it. Many times, I would open up the door and look in. There was a black bag in the closet, and I wanted to get it, but it was dark in there and I was scared to go in.

I went to my daddy and said, "Daddy, there is a big black bag in the upstairs closet. Will you please get it for me?"

He said, "Dan Dee, that room probably has mice in it. We had better not go in there."

I said, "Oh, Daddy, I want to see what is in that big black bag!"

My adventure never was a success in that closet, because Daddy would not get the bag out for me to look inside. I have always been curious about things, and I will never forget that I didn't get to look inside that big black bag. I thought it might have money in it.

I had another adventure that was about money. The next adventure was close to our house. There were some men tearing down an old grocery store. Inquisitive as I was, I went to watch them. I noticed some coins along the baseboards, and I had a feeling something exciting was about to happen.

I began to play with the coins and I asked the workers if I could have them. They said, "Yes, you can have them. You found them, cutie, so they are all yours." I became really excited and ran to show my daddy. I asked him if I could go to the store and buy something, and he said that I could.

I began to sing as I merrily went to the store. When I got to the store, I told the owner about the coins and he gladly took them. It was not until I married Claude that I found out that old coins are worth a lot of money. Well, I did not know that, and my daddy didn't either, because he was not a coin collector like Claude.

I saw the owner of the store at my parents' fiftieth wedding anniversary party. I asked him if he still had those coins, and he said he did. If I had only known about coins as I do today, I would still have them and I would not have spent them.

North Cleburne Baptist Church was right behind our house, and that is where we attended church. My daddy was ordained to be a minister there, and that is where I asked Jesus to come into my heart when I was nine years old. We could walk to church and school; the school was right across the street from us. It was a well-located house for all of our needs.

When Daddy was called to pastor a church in another city, we had to move and leave our elegant and comfortable home.

I knew I would miss our two-story house as well as my PaPa and Mama Miller (my grandparents); my Aunt Hattie Miller; my cousins, Brenda and Betty Stinson and Kay and Mike Basham; as well as all the other kids we played with and all our other relatives.

Miller Cousin Reunion 2006 at Gary and Charlotte's house and loved it!

We are the Miller cousins and hoping the stairway doesn't collapse. Ha!

They would come over to see us and we would have so much fun. Aunt Hattie would take us all to the show; she was a special aunt to all of us. I miss all the happy, fun times we had, but nothing can take my memories away.

One day, Aunt Hattie let us nieces' spend the night with her. She lived in an upstairs apartment, which was like living in a two-story house. As I go down memory lane, I hear the voices of my sisters, Sherry and Barbara Ann, and my cousins, Brenda and Betty, as well as my own voice.

Aunt Hattie she loved everyone we loved her too and she was tops with us.

I can hear in my memory the laughter and singing. I remember Aunt Hattie telling us, "Girls, I am going to let you all go outside and play in the leaves." We all got so excited to go out in the big yard! We ran and played in the huge piles of leaves, each of us taking scoops and scoops of leaves to throw on each other.

Then, all of a sudden, we all got very thirsty. We all knew that Aunt Hattie always had Dr. Pepper drinks in her apartment. We all chimed in and asked Aunt Hattie, "Can we have some Dr. Pepper?"

"Yes, you all can have some," she said.

We all went laughing and knowing that next we would get to eat popcorn and watch television.

Aunt Hattie is in heaven now, but we will never forget her. We will see her again, and so many others too.

I believe now that, if we had never moved away from our hometown, we wouldn't have had our future adventures—and we had lots of them. That would be another book to write. Life is a beautiful experience with people you love and never want to give up.

God is the real inspiration for the ideas that are helping me to write. His divine presence is like the act of inhaling fresh air. As I take my next breath, I have an impulse to write down the impressions I am getting. It causes a stirring of excitement and an anticipation of the things I am hearing to write. Some of the things I am now remembering are things I haven't thought about in many years.

The second two-story house I lived in was with Eddie and our daughter, Angela, on Fort Worth's south side. I will never forget when Eddie and I signed the papers to buy our first house. We were elated and excited.

That house had a huge, long lot with many trees and beautiful flowers. The houses surrounding ours were all fancy and the neighborhood was a delight to live in. Our house was the smallest in the neighborhood, but it was perfect for us.

Eddie came from the north side of Fort Worth and I came from Burleson, Texas. This was a new experience for the both of us. It was an unusual house because the kitchen and bedroom were upstairs. A living room, big closet, and extra room were downstairs.

I had fun cooking upstairs and looking out the window. You could see the neighborhood from up there, and it was like a big flower garden. We had a side door downstairs that led to the backyard, which was full of God's nature.

Since Eddie had to work out of town a lot, we bought a puppy to keep Angela and me company. The pup was very tiny and kept me busy.

Eddie and I played with Angela for our evening entertainment. She was a blessing to us.

We had to really watch Angela around the stairs, and I guess I should have been watched too. I had this thing about cleaning my house to stay busy.

Charlotte, my sister, had come to spend a week with us, which she frequently did. She got to witness one of my unplanned acrobatic trips down the stairs. One day, after I had finished vacuuming upstairs, I lost my balance and took a tumble all the way down the stairway. I said, "My goodness, I am falling down the stairs too quickly!"

Angela, who never left my side, was close behind me, and she was rolled up like a ball. Because of her rolled-up position, she was not hurt in the fall. Thank God that neither of us was injured, but I was extremely shaken. From then on, I tried to be very careful while vacuuming.

This house had no secret things to explore. It was a chic, fashionable, house that was built in a unique neighborhood and well cared for, which impressed me.

I loved taking Angela out in the front yard and letting her run and play. One day, I told Angela, "We are not alone. We have all these pretty flowers to keep us company." She just laughed and hugged me.

The house was set on the back part of the lot, unlike most houses, which are on the front of the lot. I wondered why the first owners did not build more. I always imagined having a long swimming pool built on the lot for all of us to enjoy.

I read my Bible and prayed often in our quaint, two-story house. It was a time in my life when I found myself needing to draw closer to God. I did not know I would soon be a widow.

I studied a Bible that my parents had bought for me when I was sixteen. With a red pen, I would underline words that spoke directly to me. This was the only Bible I had at that time. I still have it, but now I have numerous Bibles.

No matter what I ever faced, I would always turn to my Bible. I would read it until I found the Scripture for my need and then claim those words until I received peace. This gave me evidence that God had the answer to my needs.

I will always remember things that happened in that house, including the meals we shared, our daughter, our puppy, and each other downstairs in our living room.

The upstairs kitchen windows, from which I could see the sky, were a source of fascination. I would pray and I could imagine the spiritual part of me soaring like the eagles when they fly high in the sky. Since then, I have soared spiritually. The knowledge I had then does not compare to what I have now.

What a satisfaction that Eddie, Angela, and I were able to enjoy our time in this house. This was a wonderful season in our lives. I never thought I would write about it in a book.

This is the identification of this chapter: to share my meaningful life with two men, Eddie and Claude, in two, two-story houses, and to recollect the exact circumstances of our lives together. They both loved and took care of me and our children. For each of my marriages, we lived in a two-story house.

Reflecting on those houses and times has brought back to me the importance of the wedding vow "until death do us part." The Bible teaches me that God has ordered all things according to His own purpose.

My role in life now is to accept God's appointments and enjoy my life as He gives it to me. The happiness and pleasures of my past can only be understood and have lasting value as I relate it to God blessing me. My past and present are essential in making my future life worthwhile.

The third two-story house I lived in was with Claude, Angela, Claudanna, and Claude Jr. We had lived in another house in the same city before we bought this one, but we needed a bigger house because of the three children. We began looking for houses with the help of our Realtor, Leannett Johnson. She took us to look at many houses, but we could not find a house that we felt comfortable in and satisfied with.

I began to pray. I asked Jesus, "Will you help us find a house?" Soon after I asked Him, I had a vision. I saw the inside of a house; there was a room with a fireplace, and it had a white kitchen bar. I shared this vision with Claude and the children and we all believed it would happen—and it did.

When we first saw our house, we were on the bus ministry going door-to-door to invite children to church. That Saturday, we had been going up and down the streets asking parents if their children could ride the bus with us to church.

As we walked by a house, it caught both Claude's and my attention at the same time. We took down the phone number from the FOR SALE sign and called when we got home. We made an appointment to see it at 2:00 p.m. that same day.

I had some requirements for a home, which included a gas connection for my gas stove, a bedroom for each of our children, a big bedroom for Claude and me, a patio, a den, and many closets and cabinets.

The second owner of this house met us there. As he opened the door, we liked what we saw. This had not happened at any other house. I had really given up on finding the perfect house until I had the vision.

As the owner was taking us on a tour, we walked into the kitchen and den combination and I saw a white bar and the fireplace—just as I had seen in the vision. I told Claude and the children, "This is the vision I saw!" To see the fulfillment of that was exceedingly remarkable. Our children became excited and said, "Dad, Mom's vision really came to pass!"

The supernatural power of God gave me the picture of the home that we would live in for the next thirty years. We were astonished too, when the owner said, "Here is the electric, built-in oven and countertop burners, and, by the way, if you have a gas appliance, here is a place for it."

It was a perfect fit for my big gas stove! I said, "Wow." I started jumping up and down and said, "Thank you, God!"

This is why my house is so special to me, and of course also because of all the other memories I have here.

God planned this house for us, and how sweet that was of Him! I have used both the electric and gas stoves, especially when I cook for the holidays. They both come in very handy for my time in the kitchen. All my requirements were met and even more.

I talked to Jerry and Bettye Wilson, the first owners of our house. They were the couple who had the house built. They shared with me details of the extra things they added to the house, even the size of the boards that were used to build it.

Our house was very well planned and in good condition. The original owners moved because they wanted a smaller place. We needed a bigger place and God blessed us with it.

We remodeled through the years. I enjoy redecorating. We opened up the wall in the living room and made it an open space into the kitchen. We added a screened-in back porch, which reminds me of the first two-story house I lived in with my parents. I had enjoyed the screened-in porches as a child, so I wanted one in our house here.

We have a sidewalk around the back of our house and I really enjoy it. Jim, our son-in-love, installed in our front yard lights that go around the perimeter of our house, and they really complement the look at night.

We had our fireplace extended out so we would have a long place to sit in front of the fire. We had a huge den built. We have a big-screen TV, two couches, a loveseat, two armchairs, a rocking chair, a long coffee table with matching end tables, a piano, all kinds of tables, and a beautiful cabinet that came from England—all in the den. It is a very enjoyable room when we have a lot of company.

I even like to be in the den, if I am here by myself, to watch my big-screen television. We have had many parties in there.

My sister, Charlotte, gave us the cabinet from England. She lived there for a while and brought it back with her. This is the same cabinet where I put Claude's knives, watches, pens, and collections, and it makes a nice display for them. How sweet of her to give me this cabinet, which has enhanced my den.

Claude and I had the huge downstairs bedroom with three closets. I have a king-size bed, dresser, two night stands, computer desk, business desk, two recliner chairs, a beautiful chair of my mother's, and my mother's big, standing jewelry box in our bedroom.

Upstairs is my prayer room with a big window. It used to be Angela's room. Claudanna's bedroom is now a guest bedroom. Claude Jr.'s bedroom has been converted into a special room where I keep things that belonged to Claude.

My yellow bathroom—the one I call my "sunshine room"—is upstairs. I was amazed when I had the workers put in a new bathtub and they took off the shower doors. It opened up the room, and the yellow tile that you never could see was intensified by the huge mirror facing the tile.

I had just wanted to see the pretty tile, and I never took showers up there like the children had, so I did not need the shower doors. Taking them off really has made a difference. You don't even have to turn on a light in there during the day. The room just shines a pretty yellow.

I have decorated that room with many yellow things, including my mother's pretty yellow lamp. Her lamp gives the room a special touch, and it adds one more memory to my house.

I hope you can imagine the beauty of my yellow bath transformation, especially when the sun comes through the window. Like the song says, "So let the sun shine in, face it with a grin, open up your heart and let the sun shine in!" As I do what the song says, it brings the Son of God's presence and I get so blessed.

The downstairs bathroom was Claude's. We decided to have the bathtub removed and replaced with a huge shower that had a seat made for me. The shower doors look like musical notes and people have commented to me that it looks like a movie star's shower.

It was created for my hero, who was a movie star to me. I decorated it with the theme of the ocean, which he dearly loved.

When I look at that room now, I remember the man whom it was made for and I miss him so much. I do not allow myself to indulge in self-pity, or I would not be able to live here. I have to breathe in the new and remember that Claude is in my future.

I had those precious years with a wonderful a man, and I have this house because he took care of me royally.

We had beautiful tile put on our kitchen and living room floors. It shines all the time. People ask me, "Do you get on your hands and knees and clean your ceramic tile?"

I just say, "No, the tile just shines on its own, and that's why I bought it." The tile is an added touch to our special home.

As I sit here typing and reminiscing, it touches my heart that God would plan my future to be in this house debt free, peaceful, and safe. I am sure I have a cheerful expression on my face, because I feel myself smiling, and that is a good thing.

I have made up my mind to laugh and find things to laugh about. It is becoming a habit and such a natural thing that I don't even know I am doing it until someone tells me.

The other day, when I was in the beauty shop getting my hair washed, I thought of something funny and started to laugh. I knew that there were people talking about someone having a problem, but I was in my own little world. I just thought of something funny and I laughed. Later, the lady who had been washing my hair, Pat Young, said, "Something sparked in you and made you laugh."

I said, "Yes, it just came out, and it was not because of what anyone was saying. It just came out suddenly, because I was thinking of a funny thing."

The Bible says to think on good things and I try to do that, so I will live above my circumstances.

I have used Scripture, pictures, and good confessions to decorate my home, and as I pass by them I read them out loud. I personalized the passages for myself. This builds my faith for whatever I have to do or need.

My home, my family, and my life are built on a sound and good foundation. The rooms of our house are filled with precious memories and possessions. God gives me possessions and the power to enjoy them, and I accept my appointed place. This is the gift of God to me.

I will try to walk in my house in integrity, where I long to act as I should. There is a price to pay for sin but a blessing to come for doing right. I do enjoy the Word of God on the walls of my house. As for me and my house, we shall serve the Lord.

My house shall stand with God, and I will take my rightful place on this earth—and the Lord will help me endure.

The Lord cares for the possessions of the widow. I have no debts except the debt of love for others. Our house will be the inheritance from their father to my children.

I remember when Claude carried me across the threshold of our house. As he sat me down, our life began in a house that would bring us so many happy times.

Your home is like a haven to get away from all the things of the world. After you shut the doors, you have the serenity of just you and your family.

Our hearts were adorned with lace and filled with love, never to forget our times together. As a wife and mother, I was very proud of my family; they were my silks of fine quality.

Claudanna, Angela and Claude Jr. enjoyed our times of prayer together.

When they were young, Angela, Claudanna, and Claude Jr. gave us a plaque that says, "A Family That Prays Together Stays Together"—and we have. Habakkuk 2:2–3 says, "Write the vision, and make it plain." The Word of God does work, and we need to work the Word of God too.

I think God gave Claude and me an eagle's eye to have the ability to watch and observe our family and maintain the reputation of an eagle, to be father and mother figures and to show our children that love can last forever. I think their plaque proved they believed that. I still have it on my wall. Claude and I gave Angela, Claudanna, and Claude Jr. each a surprise birthday party, when they turned sixteen, here at our house. We all had a lot of fun. We always had all kinds of parties going on.

Our children all grew up too fast, and it was hard to let them go when they got married. Our babies became adults, and we had to release them to their mates. I still miss them and our times together, especially the many times we talked. I know all moms go through the same thing.

Claude and I went to a home group at church one night. There was a handsome young man there named Doug. I heard the Holy Spirit tell me, in an audible voice, that he would be Angela's husband in the future. When I got home, I told Angela. She said, "Mom!" So I let it go at that.

The other home group leaders were moving, so we decided to start a home group in our house. The first one to arrive on the first night was Doug, and he continued to attend—and of course Angela was at the home group too.

One day, Angela came to me and told me she'd had a dream. She said, "Mom, I had a dream that Doug and I got married and we were both were wearing white!" I was glad God had revealed that to her in a dream, because He had revealed it to me too. I was an overprotective mom, and God had let me know He had His stamp of approval on their love.

They began to date, and the rest is history. Angela wore a white wedding dress and Doug wore a white suit, just like in Angela's dream. They are a wonderful couple, and we have two beautiful, precious granddaughters—Bethany and Aylisa—and two handsome, precious grandsons—Caleb and Austin—thanks to Doug and Angela.

Our house has played an important part in our lives, and that is what houses should do. Doug's parents, Don and Lillian MacLeod, and the rest of his family became good friends to us. We shared a lot of happy times together.

Claudanna was reminiscing with me the other day about when Jim, her husband, asked her to marry him. They were here at our house. Jim did the proper thing: he went to Claude and asked him for Claudanna's hand in marriage. Claude approved of their marriage and blessed them. Neither Claudanna nor I knew this had happened.

Then Jim went to Claudanna and asked her to marry him. She told me later, "Mom, I went into my bathroom and stayed there for fifteen minutes before I gave him my answer!" She did accept his proposal. When they told me, I was so happy for them.

She was very particular about whom she dated. One day she had asked me, "Mom, when is the right one ever going to come into my life?" I told her just be patient and that God would bring the right one for her—and God did.

They are a wonderful couple and their union has given Claude and me two beautiful, precious granddaughters—Lauren and Andrea—and a handsome, precious grandson named Jeremy.

Lauren and Jeremy became proud parents of, Dorian Ray, their new son and our new great grandson on January 12, 2012. They chose his middle name, Ray, after his great grandfather Claude's middle name. What an honor they bestowed upon the memory of Claude.

I will never forget the day we were at church and an usher seated Jim next to us. I told Claudanna he was very handsome and she said, "Mom!"

After church he asked me if he could visit Claudanna one day at our house. I said he could, because I had a mother's intuition that Jim was meant for Claudanna. Even though I had many questions for Jim, he was a gentleman and took the time to answer them. Bless his sweet heart, he let me, the mom, be a mom.

I knew the Holy Spirit had revealed this information to me about both of my daughters. Jim's parents, Duane and Laura Sanner, and his whole family became our good friends. We all shared many happy times together too.

Claude Jr. brought beautiful Melanie to our house so we could meet her. She had long, gorgeous, blonde hair—and how sweet she is! I was amazed at her beauty and personality, and I loved her hair. Claude Jr. picked out a good Christian young lady for himself.

As time passed, they wanted to get married, and we blessed them.

We had a big meal at our home to celebrate their engagement. Melanie became a daughter to us and added a special touch to our home and family. I will never forget watching them at the altar when they were getting married. I could see their love radiating to each other.

I knew Melanie was the one for him and their love was so strong for each other. They gave us our beautiful, precious granddaughter, Tessa Jayne, who has long, pretty hair like her mom.

Melanie gave me an angel that plays the song, "Wind beneath My Wings." I had recorded this song on a CD and they played it at Claude's funeral. This touched me because it showed that she knows my heart, just like my other daughters do. Melanie has helped me on numerous insurance decisions I have had to make, and she knows her business.

Jerry and Becky Lunsford, Melanie's parents, James and Wanda Lee Reynolds, Melanie's grandparents, and her whole family became good friends to us, and we shared a lot of happy times together too.

My children married into remarkable families. We all have grown to love each other. I could not have asked for better families for my children. What a blessing for my grandchildren to have a good heritage! We all have been at many places together, and I treasure every one of those memories.

One day when I was upstairs praying in my prayer room, I heard God say, "Higher than the sky, deeper than the ocean are my plans for you, even throughout eternity. The biggest house is yet to come to you. It will be your mansion in heaven. Your other houses cannot compare to the mansion I have prepared for you."

That day, looking out my prayer window, I watched the leaves fall from the trees and knew they could never go back onto the trees again. It is like a part of my life has changed and I will never walk there again.

I know there will be new doors of opportunities that open as I am stepping into the new and letting go of the old. I sensed boldness and a tenacity coming forth in me to do things I have never done, things I should do, can do, and need to do. I am determined to walk by faith and not by sight with each step I take.

My church, Oasis, sent me a beautiful Thomas Kinkade card with a picture of a two-story house on it and the Scripture Isaiah 32:18, which says, "My people will live in peaceful dwelling places." What a blessing that was to me, especially as I have been writing my chapter on two-story houses and they mailed this card to me.

I had told my pastors, Floyd and Michelle Ellsworth, I was going to take a sabbatical to finish writing my book. It was so sweet of them to send me that particular card and at the perfect time. I had not told them the names of my chapters that I would be working on.

God is good. He knows how to speak to people, and they know how to hear him. The card was confirmation to me that I was to write the chapter on two-story houses.

It will be one year since Claude was promoted to heaven. Angela and Claudanna are coming to spend a few days with me during this time. We are going to hold onto each other, and we will get through it. We are going to visit the gravesite, and each one of us will let a balloon with a note to Claude go up in the sky.

The Lord our God will give us joy as we take pleasure honoring Claude as we stay together in our home, the place we shared with our precious husband and dad.

Chapter · Twelve

HEALING OF MY WOUNDED SPIRIT

O NE DAY, I BEGAN TO REALIZE that my spirit was wounded and that I needed to do something about it.

I had been praying about some areas in my life. I have used the Scripture Proverbs 18:14 for years when I had pain somewhere in my body. This time I was using it to search into my own spirit.

I was considering my ways and why I felt the way I did. I had a sense that something was wrong in my spirit man, and at this time I had no pain in my body. Then I decided to take a second sabbatical to continue writing more of my book.

I wanted to hear from God, and I knew that by doing a sabbatical I would hear from God.

I had suppressed, deep down in my spirit, the loss of my two husbands, even though I thought I had dealt with the loss. It was good for me to find out that I needed to deal with it again.

I am not talking about something you can see on the surface. It is something that tries to restrain you and hold you captive from deep in your spirit. I would never have known this unless the Spirit of God had revealed it to me.

I had a choice: I could either go backward or go forward with my life and be an over comer. I had to go beyond the natural to the supernatural power of God to discern my own spirit. This has been such a revelation to me. Seeking the truth has set me free.

God saw ahead and knew He wanted me to share with others who had gone through the same thing I had. He wanted them to know that there is a lady who made it, and they can make it too.

At times this past year, I would tell myself that I was just dreaming and that I would wake up soon. It was like Claude was at work or playing dominoes with his Bell Helicopter friends. I would think, *He will be home any time now.* But he never came home. And then I would come back to reality.

I would then ask God this question: "Why, God am I left here alone?" I had left that same question deep in my subconscious mind so I would not have to deal with it when I was eighteen years old.

Now, forty-five years later, I know that I should have dealt with this many years ago, but I did not know how to do it until now. I know it is God's plan for me to walk this out, so He can get all the glory.

I have taken refuge under the wings of my Lord, and He has kept me. He has lifted me up to safety to become strong and to soar above my circumstances, just like eagles soar with their wings above the clouds in the sky.

If I did not have my hope in what Jesus did for me, I would not have anything to look forward to. I have to totally lean on Jesus, or I would lose it. He does show me the next step to take, and if I miss it for that day He will show me again and I will press on.

I decided to do a sabbatical and to watch Eagle Mountain International Church with pastors George and Terri Pearsons. These were the Sunday and Wednesday services I watched on my computer. I had done the same thing when I had my first sabbatical. This was where Claude and I had been going to church when he went to be with Jesus.

After my first sabbatical ended, I started going to Oasis Community Worship Center because it is closer to my home. Pastors Floyd and Michelle gave their blessing to me in writing my book, and I have felt their prayers. It is so sweet of them to be so supportive.

As I am writing this chapter, I am hearing God so clearly. He is telling me I have never really gotten to the root of the death of my first husband, Eddie, and now I have to deal with Claude's death. By that, I mean that

I have not come to terms with how Eddie's death caused my spirit to be wounded. I was not aware of this until right now as I am typing.

Yes, I have had the Word spoken over me. I have danced, sung, and worshipped God, and it has really helped me. But I have not dealt with my wounded spirit because I didn't know what the problem was—until now.

According to Proverbs 17:22 (AMP), "A happy heart is good medicine and a cheerful mind work's healing, but a broken spirit dries up the bones."

Last month, my doctor ordered a bone-density test. It revealed that I need to take pills for my bones, and this confirmed to me that my spirit was broken. This is a total revelation to me. I know that God has spoken to my heart. Now I can deal with it and start to recover in my spirit and my bones.

I do not want my spirit to be broken. I want it to be strong and alert, and I want to also have healthy bones. I know God has a purpose for me to fulfill.

According to Proverbs 25:28 (AMP), if I don't have rule over my own spirit, then it will be like a city that is broken down and without walls.

Before I realized my spirit was wounded, I had been confessing these Scriptures.

Matthew 10:26 (KJV) – "For there is nothing covered, that shall not be revealed and hid that shall not be known."

Luke 8:17 (KJV) – "For nothing is secret, that shall not be made manifest, neither anything hid that shall not be known."

1 Corinthians 2:10 – "God will unveil and reveal through His Spirit anything hidden in our lives."

When I lost a bracelet, I started confessing these Scriptures because I knew God would help me find it. God had a plan for me to do this, and He began to reveal other things to me. I did find my bracelet, and I was so glad.

In my past experiences, God would bring something to the surface that I needed to deal with because He knew that I was ready.

God's grace and mercy are so wonderful. God reveals things to me sometimes that are beyond my own scrutiny, because I never knew those things existed. It is in the deepest part of my spirit that they were hidden.

When God has me to deal with a situation, He will give me a Scripture, a dream, or a thought, or I will hear a sermon. It will be revealed however He chooses to show me.

I have a plaque in my kitchen window that says, "Grace is when God gives me what I don't deserve and mercy is when God doesn't give me what I do deserve." This makes me feel graced with gratitude, wisdom, love, compassion, and forgiveness.

I like to remind myself that God is there for me even if I don't do everything perfectly. In my stomach, I began to have pain that would not go away. I knew Proverbs 18:14 (KJV): "The spirit of a man will sustain his infirmity; but a wounded spirit who can bear it?" I began to meditate on that Scripture.

I still had not realized that my spirit had been wounded for a long time. I began to consider my ways and what had come to me. I tried to think of something lately that had happened or something I had done that I needed to deal with, and I began to deal with some things. Needless to say, I was hurting, and I knew that my spirit was wounded.

I called some people to pray for me, and I went to bed with a heating pad on my stomach. When Sunday came, I turned on my computer to watch the EMIC church service. When Pastor George started preaching, he gave the title of his sermon and a Scripture to accompany it. To my amazement, the Scripture was Proverbs 18:14 and the sermon title was, "How to Develop a Strong Spirit."

No one can tell me that this was not God speaking to me. Wow! I knew that I would have a complete healing in my spirit from the loss of two husbands as well as the healing of my bones.

Pastor George is going to do a series on this subject on Wednesday nights, and that will be a big blessing to me. I will be able to watch it on my computer too. Praise God! He knew I needed this.

And by the way, I have no more pain and I am healed. It is like the revelation of all of this stopped the pain. Of course, Jesus paid the price for me, and He gets all the credit for me not having any more pain.

I would have never known Pastor George was teaching on this if I had not decided to take my second sabbatical. I seized the opportunity to seek God and I began to confess daily that my steps are ordered of the Lord, and He did order them.

I now have the complete understanding of how the plan of God for my life is unfolding right before my eyes. I have taken hold of what I have in my hand at this time in my life. I have a quiet place where I can write and hear from God. I don't have to go to a job, so I can concentrate on writing my book.

I feel very blessed to be able to have the freedom to do this. It is not just for me but for all of those who need to be healed in their spirit as I did.

I have listened to Keith Moore's CDs on "How to Develop a Strong Spirit," so I have heard two good teachings on this subject. God is allowing what I have had to deal with to enlighten me on this subject. It is happening in a way that only the Spirit of God has allowed to surface.

A friend, Howard Meister, did a very sweet thing for me. He brought me the Word Search 9 program to help me as I am studying and preparing my book. He also gave me some CDs of Pastor Floyd's sermons from the last few weeks. That was a very thoughtful thing for Howard to do.

The title of Pastor Floyd's sermon was, "That's What I Long For." When I finished listening to the first CD, the Spirit of the Lord said to me, "This will be part of the healing of your spirit."

Tears began to fill my eyes as I realized my spirit had been wounded from losing my husbands. It was not that they had rejected me, but I felt I had done something to cause this to happen. This had been affecting my spirit, but I had not recognized it. God designed a longing to be loved in all of us.

As Pastor Floyd said, "The longings are like an aching in your heart to be loved." For me, it was because my spirit was wounded. He also said, "Don't assign the rejection to a person or situation, because it is an attack of the enemy." I had let the enemy use the weapon of rejection to wound my spirit.

I know that the condition of my bones did not develop overnight. It has been a process that has occurred in my body over a period of time. You know what? I am a fighter, but I can only fight against the enemy after his approach has been discovered.

I claim I am healed by the stripes that Jesus bore for me.

I remembered the Bible talked about the widow being grieved. Isaiah 54:4 (KJV) says, "A widow shall forget the shame of her youth and not remember the reproach of her widowhood anymore." I knew as I read this that, deep in my spirit, I hadn't released the reproach of it all.

It brings a feeling of rejection that the one who loved you is gone and you are left to raise your baby all alone. I realized, after listening to Pastor Floyd's sermon, that the enemy had made me think I was too young to successfully raise a baby without a husband. The feeling was that of being inadequate and abandoned by someone who loved me, even though it was not his fault at all that he died.

I had most definitely pushed this feeling deep into my spirit. I had suppressed it into my subconscious so I would not have to deal with it. And that was forty-five years ago.

I know that the bone test proved my spirit was wounded. This was the key to open the door of my deliverance. Everything I have done, listened to, or watched spiritually has taught me to seize these moments.

I also asked the Holy Spirit if there were any bitter-root judgments that I have made about someone and asked Him to reveal them to me. I began to hear things I needed to repent of: the people in my past that had hurt me, whether it was a teacher, a friend, family members, situations, or whatever. I have always been a repentant person, but these were things I had suppressed. I did not realize they were still there. Only the Holy Spirit could reveal them to me.

I knew I had met the enemy of my soul head on, and I discerned the tactics he used to cause my spirit to be wounded. I repented of any bitter-root judgments I had made.

According to Matthew 16:19, Jesus gave us the keys of the kingdom of heaven to bind the evil and loose the good. When I repented, the binding and loosing began. I bound the strongman and I commanded the spirit of rejection to get away from me and never bother me again in the name of Jesus.

I loosed myself to be free and go on with my life, forgetting my past and pressing on to my future. I broke the curse me with the blood of Jesus and the cross of Jesus Christ. It was only by the power of the Holy Spirit and Pastor Floyd's sermons that I have discerned what those things were.

I have a teaching that I do on the generational curses that God will let surface in your life whenever you are ready to deal with an issue. I have come to a place in my life where what I teach is being proven.

Since I have dealt with these issues, God has allowed a special incident to happen to me. Of all times for this to happen, it was when I was putting on my makeup. The night before, I had been invited to a party. I told the hosts I would let them know the next day if I was coming. As I was putting on my makeup, I heard this clicking sound.

Something clicked three times. As I told you before there is something about the number three that God uses in my life.

I turned to see where the sound was coming from. All of a sudden, my music box, which the Daystar Prayer Department had given me when my mother went to heaven, began to play "Amazing Grace."

I said, "Oh, my goodness! How did that start playing?" I realized that an angel of the Lord had turned the wind-up key and made it play.

I then asked God, "What are you trying to tell me through this?" I got quiet before the Lord and listened for Him to tell me.

Then God said, "I want you to go to the party and grace a certain person with love."

It was a wonderful way for God to reveal to me that I should go, and it was so exciting to know that the angels were with me and helping me make the decision. It must have been very important for God to let my music box play. I will always be grateful He cares so much for each one of us.

The other day, Howard gave me a prayer that he prays over me and other people. This is the prayer: "My prayer for you and every living human being is that heaven would give you dreams, visions, audible voices, and angelic visitations so you will know the truth and heaven's reality and what heaven has for you to do."

I can say that the angels did visit me, and that is so neat! I believe God heard Howard's prayer. I feel so honored that God would do that, because I know this truly means I am not alone, for the angels are watching over me and encamped around me.

Thank you, Howard, for praying for me and giving me your prayer.

I am so grateful to Pastor George Pearsons, Pastor Keith Moore, and Pastor Floyd Ellsworth for teaching and ministering to me at this perfect time in my life.

I can see that my book was written for the healing of my past and to share with others. My God amazes me that He cares enough for me to walk me through this life and to teach me so I can teach others.

I know I can't live by my senses, but I have to let the Holy Spirit lead me. My conduct must be controlled and guided by Him too.

There is a Scripture for every need that I will ever have; I just have to seek God and experience His presence. I may have to hit the pause button sometimes, as I have done by taking a sabbatical, in order to hear from God.

Sometimes, I may need to fall on my face and call on God, especially when the heat is on. I need to acknowledge Him in my life and tell Him how faithful He is and that I know that He is ordering my steps.

I am learning that loneliness is not an enemy. It is a solitary place without other people around me. It is where I can draw closer to God and receive instruction from heaven, and this is the purpose for it. I realize I am never alone except in my mind, and I have the angels making things work that I know only the angel of the Lord could do. It has become very exciting for me. I anticipate every day for the supernatural in my life and home.

Do you remember when I asked God why I had been left alone? Well, what I have heard and seen in my home has made me realize that God is with me. I always have known that, but now I have experienced it.

The angels are with me, and I know there will be doors opening up in my life to fulfill my destiny. I know it will never happen though, until I have drawn as close as I can to God. He has been waiting a long time for me to do just that.

Being retired and debt free, I can make sure that I do take the time God wants me to spend with Him. Jesus is my best friend, and as I fellowship with Him in my time of loneliness I will walk right into my destiny.

As I embrace this truth, then loneliness is a good thing. I will not let it break me. It will empower me to be like an eagle flying high above any circumstance in my life.

Praise God! He has allowed me to see why I am alone. It is not because I have done something wrong but because I have a calling on the inside of me that God has planned. He wants me to hear directly from Him. He wants to let me know the plans that were designed especially for me before I was even in my mother's womb.

I realized that I have a calling on my life but also that I had to first surrender my life. My surrendering was not to let go of God, it was to run to Him. He is after my heart, just as He was in the emergency room with Claude.

I told God, "I love Claude with all my heart, but I love you God more." I knew God wanted me to draw closer to Him. I didn't draw close enough though, or I would not have gone through all the loneliness and fear. I should have let God's love embrace me and I should have surrendered to a quiet, resting place at Jesus's feet.

I am now seeing my future through my spiritual eyes and I have decided to live there. I can see myself showing other people how I have walked through and have become the victor.

I know it takes people who have been set free to set others free. I want to tell people that Jesus loves them and that He will do for them what He has done for me. When Jesus sets a person free, he or she is free indeed.

All of us need privacy and a relationship with our Maker, God. I know I can't be God for my life. I have to draw away to God, even if I am not on a sabbatical, and trust Him. A single day in God's court is better that being anywhere else. God gave Jesus to all of us, and I am glad I accepted Him when I was a small child so I could lean on Him. I love every minute I spend with my God, and I enjoy His presence, as I know all of you do.

It has been a process for me to get where I am today, and look at all the numerous people God has blessed me with! They have graced my life through my journey. I am so grateful for each one individually, people who wrote their tender words in my heart when I was hurting. The days they spoke to me are the best days of any of those years, and I have gained joy from them.

I have had to become strong in the broken places of my life, and I have scooped them up and laid them at the feet of Jesus. The brokenness has brought me to the end of myself and has brought a special grace from God's all-surpassing power to make me stronger.

I don't see how anyone can make it in this life if they don't trust in what Jesus did for them. Jesus paid a big price for me, and I can't let what He did for me be in vain.

I can be an overcomer and so can you. I have to hold my head up and believe I can soar in life like the eagles do. They fly high in the sky with strength in their wings that God has given them.

Healing has come to me, and it makes me want to sing, sing, sing and dance, dance, dance.

When God gave me a passion to write this book, He gave me the expressions and concept to do it. God gave me free access to approach Him. I would sit down at my computer and say, "Wisdom, give me the words to write." And He did.

Hearing God's voice is as simple as quieting my own self down, fixing my eyes on Jesus, allowing spontaneity, and beginning to write. Writing down the flow of thoughts becomes very exciting as they light up my mind.

I am discovering the peace that can only come by doing something I enjoy. It's as if I ask God, "What dream do you have for my future?" I then let Him reveal my future with a pen in my hand as a ready writer.

As I began to write from my heart on different subjects, it becomes timely advice to others.

I am now healed in the deepest part of my soul, which has escalated to the outside surface. Totally free inside and outside to go places and do things that God has planned for me before the foundation of the earth.

There is nothing hidden anymore to hold me back and to keep me in a place that I didn't even realize was there. The truth has set me free from all the things that drew me to a wounded spirit. I can have new expectations in my life and press forward and not backward.

I am convinced that nothing can separate me from the love of God. I am very particular about what I read, watch, and hear, because it is feeding my spirit. We are what we eat and ponder on, and some things are laced with stuff we cannot even taste because the enemy has covered them up.

If it's good for me, I will like it, and if it is bad for me, I will dislike it. I will now hit the pause button when I need to hear from God and hit the delete button when the enemy tries to use a weapon against me.

The opening of God's Word gives me quick understanding. I want to learn not just to stand but to walk.

God, create in me a cleanness of heart and mind, so my eyes can become the windows of my soul. I will not boast and feel superior because I will remember I am only a part of God's tree. I am not a root, only a branch, because Jesus is the root that supports me.

Lord Jesus, move upon every reader with waves of love and peace. Rest upon them and breathe upon them so that they can find their rightful place in this world.

The breath of You, God, has given me the desire to go on with my life. I'm expecting it to be exciting and happy. It has inspired me to write this book and be pleasing to you.

Chapter Thirteen

NEW INSPIRED TRADITIONS

I HAVE STARTED SOME NEW TRADITIONS, SO I can look forward to each special time of every year and do again the things I did, either by myself or with others. To me, establishing traditions is an adventure, and it takes my mind to happy things.

God gives me blessings, but happiness is up to me. I know what it is to be without someone whom you loved so very much. I have to keep calm and carry on with my life, keep my faith strong for what I hope for. I will believe God will see me through.

On Claude's and my first wedding anniversary since he had gone to heaven, I decided to write a note to Claude and attach it to a balloon. I wanted to let it go at Claude's graveside. My daughter, Claudanna, and my sister, Charlotte, went with me. I began to sing, "Happy anniversary" to Claude. Then I said, "Jesus, will you take the balloon straight up to heaven, to Claude?" I let the balloon go and it shot into the sky and disappeared fast.

I believe Jesus did hear my request. That just tickles me. I think Jesus made it possible for me to rejoice and have "joy unspeakable and full of glory," as in 1 Peter 1:8. I am determined to be happy and enjoy my blessings. I want to do this every year on our anniversary in the future.

Claude once bought me a stuffed bunny rabbit that could say, "Tickle, tickle, wiggle, wiggle, that tickles me!" I picked it up the other day, hugged it, and then walked away because I knew it didn't work anymore. As I walked away, it said, "That tickles me!" I started laughing. I loved that moment; it was a "suddenly" moment. I believe my angel had a part in that moment. That is why I can say "that tickles me." I am expecting a lot of things to make me happy, according to Romans 15:13.

By the way, maybe the bunny rabbit just needs some fresh batteries. As I have shared,

I was spoiled by Claude. I never put batteries in things because he always did that.

Right now, I am off to get some batteries. Let's see if that will keep my bunny rabbit talking all the time.

Well, I am back. I got the bunny rabbit some batteries. I thought I had found where to replace the batteries. I cut a string off, and its tail fell off! I said, "Oh, my goodness, I cut the bunny's tail off!"

I still have not found anywhere to replace any batteries.

Hey, Howard just drove up to my house. He's going with me to the store to buy parts to replace my circuit-breaker box. I will ask him to help me.

I am going to answer the door. "Come on in, Howard, and let's go to the kitchen," I said. Then I immediately ask him, "Can you help me find a place to replace the batteries for my stuffed rabbit? I would like to do this before we go to the store."

Well, of course he said, "Yes." He found it and showed me how to put the batteries in. I said, "Thank you, Howard. You are a blessing. You can fix anything!"

The bunny rabbit works great now. I did sew the rabbit's tail back on and I got a big laugh from listening to it and watching it. I will be pressing the button a lot to hear it, because it really makes me laugh!

I will pray that the "God of my hope" will always fill me with joy and peace.

I believe all the experiences I will have in the future will do this. By the power of the Holy Spirit, I will always abound and be overflowing with a bubbling of joy and hope.

People are always saying to me, "You are so happy and you are always smiling!" What I am sharing with you is how I overcame the sting of the loss of my loved ones. I have purposed in my heart and with my mouth to smile. It comes from within and then comes out and shows on my face. The glory of the Lord has risen upon me and I praise Him for it. Without God, this would not be possible.

I want my future to be better than my past. I want to have new experiences and to enjoy my life and help others to enjoy life too. I will always try to find someone who needs a good laugh, and I'll share my stories with them. Writing this book is a part of that. I want to cherish my yesterdays, live for today, and dream of my tomorrows.

I have decided to buy a funny stuffed animal like the rabbit that can make me laugh, especially for this coming November 26. That will be the anniversary of the day Claude was promoted to heaven. I want to say to my sweet Claude, "The Lord went with you the day He called you home. I do rejoice that you have made it to heaven and that one day I will go to heaven too. It did break my heart, and a part of me went with you."

I will say, "Claude, all of our children miss you and I hope what I have written in my book can bring a part of you back to them too. Our babies have turned into mature adults, but they miss and love you so much, and I do too."

It will be a new thing for me to buy a stuffed, talking animal, because I have never bought any for myself. It will be exciting to see what I will be able to find and laugh with.

We need to laugh often, love much, and live well. I am going to believe I will live forever and live like I only have today. We have to laugh like no one is listening and live like it's heaven on earth.

I want to share a note my granddaughter, Lauren Sanner Francis, wrote to me on January 1, 1999. "Nana, encourage and build up your family daily. Help them identify everything that hinders them and any sin that could so easily entangle them, pray that they will complete the race of life that God has already marked out for them, and give them courage." Lauren was only eleven years young when she wrote me the note. Now she is twenty-two years young. God does have our future planned for us, and it will be good.

As I write this book, I do want to encourage every reader, and my family, to have faith in God and watch Him open doors for you that no man can close. Lauren did not know how profound her note to me was or that it would go into my book in the future. God speaks through children, and they are all special. We can glean from their words of wisdom. We can put our life in God's hands and see what He will do in our lives.

Bethany Mitchell, my first granddaughter, recently put a picture of me on Facebook. She was participating in a Thirty-Day Challenge to post a picture of someone who inspires you on Facebook. She wrote a comment saying, "This is my Nana and she inspires me so much. She has been through a lot, but still manages to praise God, even on her worst days."

Her words so inspired me that I wanted to add them to my book. That is exactly why I am writing this book: to show people that if I can make it, they can make it too.

Everyone can make it if they praise God. Psalm 34:1 says, "I will bless the Lord my God at all times; His praise shall continually be in my mouth."

A friend of mine, Patty Wilkinson, with whom I worked at Daystar, gave me a note one day. She said, "I just want you to know that I will always remember how you taught me how to pray with people concerning different matters." She said, "Danva, you have been given a role in history, to fulfill your God-given destiny."

What a tender moment that was when she shared her feelings with me! Now she has gone to her home in heaven. None of us knew Claude and Patty would go to heaven and I would write a book sharing memories of them.

I will always be sure that I share how others have blessed my life and what they have done for me. I will make a new tradition of doing that.

Sherry Matthaei, my sister, sent me a beautiful necklace when I graduated from John Roberts Modeling School. She was not able to come to the ceremony, but I still cherish the necklace.

I stayed with Sherry during my last year of high school. She was the home economics teacher at Rio Vista High School. Sherry said that what I had learned in modeling school was the same curriculum she learned in college, and that our tests were similar too. This is the same school that Eddie came to when he proposed to me and gave me an engagement ring.

I was in my first fashion show at Rio Vista High School. Sherry taught many of us how to make the dresses that we modeled. She was a great teacher to me and her students.

This is going to be a new tradition for me: to be a better teacher of the Word of God. I will share with people in my life how to do everything that I have learned to do. I will try to encourage them just as my sister Sherry did. We don't have a promise of tomorrow, so we need to live the best we can for today.

When Claude saw the Rio Vista fashion show picture of me, he said, "This is mine!" He put it on his nightstand and always kept it there. I still have it, but I have put it away. He wanted all the pictures of me that he could get.

Now I have all these pictures of me that were his. My goal is to replace them with something to make me happy. I will set some aside for my children and keep some out. I do want to fill my walls with Scriptures, beautiful art, and positive confessions. Now I can do whatever my fancy is and redecorate some things in my home if I want to.

I am a frugal manager of money, and I do believe in staying on a budget. I will wait to buy something until I know that it can be allowed on my budget. I have no one to answer to except God, but He expects me to use wisdom.

I don't have to cook if I don't want to, and I can stay up late if I want to. I can watch my favorite television programs, go shopping, or dance on my dance floor. I can pray any time I want to, or sing, because no one is listening.

I owe no debts, except to love people. I enjoy sitting on my screened-in porch and watching the birds. I reminisce about my life with Claude and my family and think about how I can press on to my future years.

I learned many years ago that we can just believe God for those things that would go over our budget. I learned it in a financial class that Don Spears taught at Word of Faith.

Don had a lady come in and share with the class. She said if there were clothes we wanted and we did not have the money to buy them, we should go into the stores and try them on. This would encourage us to believe that God would supply the clothes and it would build our faith to trust God as our source.

The lady also did some color analysis on some people and showed them what colors would look best on them. I thought I would like to learn to do that. That was in the year 1986.

A few years later, I went to Beauti Control Cosmetics School and learned how to do it. My friend, Connie Harris, went with me. We enjoyed it so much. I went to modeling school first and then to Beauti Control School, both in the year 1990. Many people asked me, "Why do you want to go to modeling school? You are a Christian."

I said, "Well, do we need to learn how to increase our knowledge of how to dress and learn what looks best on us? Or should we look like we are from the Stone Age?"

I just had a desire to learn to be a model and an image consultant. I know that God put that desire in me. I have taught many people how to dress and do their makeup, and I have done their color analysis. I enjoyed being the master of ceremonies for fashion shows for churches and Elroy Roberts TV Productions. I never went to New York to model; I modeled only at local fashion shows or at the Apparel Mart in Dallas.

One day at Word of Faith Church, I saw this young lady. God told me to ask her if I could do her color analysis and a makeover for her. She agreed.

I went to her house in Dallas. As I finished her color analysis, she called her mother in and said, "Mom, I look just like the dream I had about myself last month!" She had thought she was not pretty and she had a low self-image. All of that was about to change.

I taught her what colors to put on her skin tone and how to apply her makeup. I shared with her that God made the skin tone we have. Just learning what colors complement our skin tone helps us look better. She was so excited about her new look and told me I looked pretty. She thanked me for taking my time to help her find the good self-image she now has.

My sister, Barbara Ann Eckhart, sent me a picture of a little girl kissing a little boy. There was another little girl watching them and she had a frown on her face. She looked like she wanted that kiss. She told me it was a picture of me kissing our cousin Larry and it was she who was frowning.

I told her I had never seen that picture before and asked her where she had gotten it, because it did look like us! That picture makes me laugh every time that I look at it.

One day, Barbara Ann called me and said it was really our sister Nancy frowning in the picture. I believed her and laughed more every time I looked at it. Then one day she called me again and said, "I was just teasing you. It wasn't really any of us." Well, I didn't care, because it still makes me laugh.

I am going to find more pictures that make me laugh and make that another one of my new traditions. I also think sisters and brothers have a closeness that makes this world a better place.

Barbara Ann and I used to sing a lot together and Sherry would play the piano. One day we were with our family in a restaurant. Some people asked my sisters Sherry, Barbara Ann, Nancy, and me if we were the Lennon sisters!

Daddy told them, "No, but thank you for the compliment." We were asked that same question at other times too. Things like that become precious memories. We grew up so fast.

I probably have not stopped long enough to take time to smell the roses. I want to make another new tradition. I will take time to smell the roses. I am writing my book and trusting God to make my tongue the pen of a ready writer.

Nancy Southard, my sister, found a beautiful meaning for Claude's name and had it framed when he retired from Bell Helicopter. The words were these: "Claude is a majestic person who has a future with no tears. His personality is bright and cheerful and genuine, light of step and heart is he. His style will leave enormous footprints. He has the ability to be a man of initiative and his character is not content with the easy. He always is willing to offer his help and has boundless energy and strength." What an excellent description of Claude!

Claude's style was always in good taste. He knew how to dress. People would tell him, "You dress like a Philadelphia lawyer." What a compliment for him! He was proud to be what his parents raised him to be.

I want to start a new tradition of finding the meaning of people's names and expressing that to them through a card or letter, like Nancy did.

Another sister, Charlotte Yeathermon, has sent me many special sayings through the years. She has also made cards on her computer for me and I have been so blessed by them. I want to do that for others, too.

I want to create special sayings that will bless people as Charlotte's have blessed me. I would like to share with you this one: "If sisters were flowers, I'd still pick you. I'd let the sun shine so you'd never be blue. I'd show the world how beautifully you grew, with bright, bold colors and strength through and through. A sister's smile warms your heart and she is a lifelong friend who cares about you."

Charlotte and Gary invited my children and me to their house last Thanksgiving Day, the day Claude went to heaven. I was so numb that I was no good to anyone and couldn't help to prepare for Thanksgiving dinner. They compassionately took us under their wings.

I believe God gave us our families, and He handpicked them for us. I am so blessed to have six sisters and one brother. Each one of them has a special place in my heart. They all were there for me when Claude was promoted to heaven. Claude was like a brother to them; they all loved him and he loved them.

Oscar Dale Curington, my brother, has been there for me during my time of healing. He took me to see my sister, Sherry. He took me also to visit my cousins, Brenda and Tommy Dodge, for their fiftieth wedding anniversary. He has taken me out to eat and other interesting places. He told me he would come to get me whenever I needed him.

I had been used to Claude doing all the driving. I was just spoiled and loved every minute of it. When he was no longer here, it was devastating to me.

Since my brother is the only boy my parents had, I think he wants to help as if they were still here. My parents were with me during every step I had to take when Eddie went to heaven.

Oscar Dale has been an undergirding for me. We stayed together the last two weeks of our mother's life, and now he is here for me, since Claude is not here. I don't have my parents or Claude to maintain balance in my life, and I miss that. It's good to have a brother. Even though I am older than he, he is still my *big brother.*

I want to make a new tradition to find creative ways to undergird others when they need it. My other sister, Phyllis Holder, gave me a Thomas Kinkade music box that plays "Amazing Grace." I keep it in my kitchen to remind me of her. I know that God will give me grace to make it.

Buying someone something like the music box is a gesture of love, and I appreciate it so much.

I want to start a new tradition of touching someone's life with something like a music box to give them comfort.

Phyllis and her husband Rick offered us such hospitality when they let us stay at their house. I know it was hard on Rick and Phyllis to have so many people in their house, but they never complained. May God always bless them for allowing us to be with our mom in her last days!

Sandra Curington, my youngest sister, is in heaven. She went suddenly, and we all miss her. Sandra was a giver. She gave me a little black purse that I use all the time when I need a smaller purse to carry. I think of her every time I use that purse. She is on my mind a lot.

I was asked to style Sandra's hair and do her makeup for her funeral, and I said I would.

My daughter, Angela, and my sister, Nancy, helped me. That was a wonderful experience. I felt angels in the room with us. I talked to her as I did her makeup, because she is alive—in her spirit in heaven. She looked like a little angel when we finished. I could see peace on her face and knew she was watching what we were doing.

Going to modeling school and beauty school gave me the skills to do this for her. I also did this for my mother's funeral.

Stephanie McCullough, my niece, helped me fix my mother's hair, and my sister Charlotte stayed in the room with us. I wanted to leave my mother's glasses off for the funeral, because when I had finished doing her makeup, I wanted her great facial features to show. Mother's glasses were laid in the casket, by request of my brother. That was a nice thing to do.

My mother was a beautiful woman. We all have a picture of her when she was in her twenties and looked like Dorothy Malone, the movie star.

I am so glad that God and Claude allowed me to go to school to learn how to do makeovers so I could do that for my mom and sister. I want to make a new tradition of doing something out of the ordinary to spice up someone's life. I want to use the creativity that God has given to me.

Angela, my daughter, suggested that when I finish my book I should start journaling, which would enhance my writing for future projects. I agreed with her. That will be one more new tradition for me.

I know that, apart from enthusiasm, joy cannot live. I have to plan things to do for myself and trust God to order my steps. All of us were born to be happy every day. Laughter is from God, and unhappiness and gloom are from the Devil.

All the things we wear should be an expression of our personality. I believe in putting your best foot forward, putting a smile on your face, and wearing the colors that are right for your skin tone. Someone can look at your face and see if you are happy or sad; wearing the right colors can show the same thing. A good way to see if you are wearing the right color is noticing if you get compliments that day.

I always tell anyone who is mad at someone, "You know all you need is some *Glad* wrap!"

Just laugh a little, sing a little as you go on your way in life, and remember that a mind unemployed is a mind not enjoyed. You know our work is a portrait of ourselves. I was taught in modeling school, "Don't go out in the public without being properly dressed, because you never know who is watching you. And for sure don't go out in rollers!"

To me, life is dealing with the sunshine and wanting to win people to Jesus. We should take the time to learn how to present ourselves to the world, if we want people to listen to us about Jesus.

As we seek happiness, it will seek us. The smile on your face is the light in your window and it shows people you are happy. People are drawn to a smile—and a well-dressed person.

There is not one cosmetic for beauty like happiness, so I say to smile all the time. Ministers Charles and Frances Hunter taught me this: "Every day, get in front of your mirror and say, 'I am beautiful because Jesus is in me' and then smile."

If you do this, people will begin to say to you, "I always see a smile on your face!" Start practicing to smile in your mirror and it will become natural to you as you go about your day.

My new tradition is to take more time to stop and tell people when I notice them smiling.

I want to make another new tradition to go places that I have never been to before. I will seek God and His direction for this. I know I will have a new kind of life because of His deep love and plan for me.

I want to set my thoughts on meditation of God's Word and hear His voice. I want to have a rich experience of knowing Jesus more and letting my roots grow deeper and deeper in Him. Then I will become strong and vigorous in the truth that He will reveal to me, and I'll let heaven fill my thoughts.

I want to go to untapped places in my life that can bring glory to God. I want to go to the places that God created for me so I can to enjoy and behold His creation. I am going to start to expect more out of heaven than I ever have before.

Last Tuesday, I went to the Sunflower Shop to get my vitamins. As I was leaving, I was drawn to the German deli next door. I had not planned to, but I felt the urge to, go in. I walked into the store and began to look at the clocks, dishes, and curios. They had all kinds of German merchandise and food. I saw a cute toy, a stuffed chicken that had a button that said PRESS. When I pressed it, music played as the chicken started to dance. I immediately started laughing. I had found my funny stuffed animal for November 26! It's a toy that will make me laugh—a singing, dancing chicken. It makes chicken noises too and does the German chicken dance.

Everyone in the store heard me laughing. I began to share with some of them that I had been looking for something like that and the reason why I wanted it. God does provide the desires of our heart.

I asked the ladies working in the store how to spell some words in German, including *thank you,* which is *Danke schoen.*

Howard, who has done so much work for me at my house, is German. I wanted to give him a thank-you note in German. He replaced my electric circuit-breaker box, which I really do appreciate. He is a master crafter at whatever he does, and he does an excellent job. Claude and I have had a lot of workers doing things at our house during the past thirty years, but Mr. Howard tops all of them.

When I took my chicken home, do you know what I did? I danced with my German dancing chicken and had a blast. When I need cheering up, I grab my chicken and set him on my dance floor. I say, "Chicken, dance with me," and we start dancing. I am sure I look funny, but it makes me laugh and no one is watching except God—and I believe Claude is watching too!

I made a plan and it happened because God ordered my steps to that German store and I found my funny stuffed animal. It is fun to plan, because I can see God open the doors for me to walk through. It is exciting too.

I am getting curious to learn more about the Germans, since God led me into the German store. I even bought a plaque of a city named Rothenburg, Germany. It is made out of the pretty, Delft-blue style from the Netherlands. Rothenberg is near the border between Germany and the Netherlands.

For years, I have decorated with the Delft blue things throughout my house. I never knew until I went into that German store what it was called. I do believe God ordered my steps to that particular store that day.

My life is getting more exciting as the days go by. I hope I am encouraging someone to get excited and know God can make life happier and better than we have ever dreamed.

I was thinking Claude's grandfather had been German. I called his sister, Wanda Woods, who confirmed that he was. She said their grandfather's name was Joe Strnad and he had been a farmer with a big farm in Kaufman, Texas. He also had a very large garden every year.

Their grandmother's name was Lucinda Haley Strnad; she was Irish. Joe and Lucinda were Zoetta's parents. Zoetta married Claude York. They had three children: Wanda, Claude, and Joe. Claude my husband was named after his dad. Joe was named after his grandfather.

This will be one of my newly inspired traditions, for now and for the future. I want to discover everything I can about my children's ancestors and also my own. I want to give them all the information I find.

I was inspired today to make a tradition of remembering the things people have given me. I want to let them know I appreciate everything they have given me, and it is still blessing me. I also want to let them know that, as I look at these things in my home, they bring me comfort in the time of my grief over the loss of Claude. What better way to let them know that than to do it in my book! I want to share some of them.

Claude, my children, and my grandchildren have given me many beautiful angels. I have collected angels through the years. I have a plaque hanging on the wall close to those angels that says, "There is joy among and in the presence of the angels of God. Luke 15:10." They remind me of all the happy times we had together.

My grandchildren gave me a plaque that says, "There Is No Place Like Home, Except Nana and Papa's House." It graces my bedroom wall and makes me feel so blessed when I see it.

Bethany, our first grandchild, named us Papa and Nana, and I have always liked those names for us. I also like my name: Danva. I am glad my parents named me this. I have never known anyone else with that name. It is a unique name, and I have my parents to thank for that.

My mother and my sister, Charlotte, gave me the most beautiful pink lamp with a matching teapot set. I will never forget how surprised I was when I received that gift. The lamp and teapot set also matched the décor of the things on the table where I placed them.

I have a big painting above the table that says, "For Me and My House We Will Serve the Lord. Joshua 24:15."

I have many paintings that grace the walls of my home that my mother painted, and I treasure her work as an artist.

My neighbors, Vernon and Patty Perry, gave Claude a Thomas Kinkade book titled *It Is Well with My Soul*. I enjoy reading that book and looking at the beautiful paintings. It still blesses me as it did him.

I can say Vernon and Patty are the best neighbors I have ever had. They take excellent care of their property and always share their gold nuggets of wisdom with me. I believe God looked down from heaven and planned for us to live right next door to each other.

In 2006, Betty Cook and Brenda Dodge had a slumber party for all the girl cousins at Betty's house. I still have the framed picture they gave to us. It says, "Families Are Forever."

As I go through my house, memories like this will always have a special place in my heart. They took the time to get us all together, and we had a wonderful time. Betty and Brenda's mother, my Aunt Sis (Retha Stinson), stayed up late with us, talking and eating.

We were surprised by a visit from Danny and David Stinson, Betty and Brenda's brothers, who thought it, would be funny to dress up like girls to give us a big laugh. They sure did make us laugh, and we enjoyed them coming.

I remember when I started working at Daystar Television. My supervisor, Mrs. Gloria Torres, said, "Danva, I want to teach you how to work on the computer." She taught me many things. What s blessing she has been to me and I do appreciate her and all she taught me. She and I became very close and we will always be good friends.

Gloria Torres and Prayer Partners with Governor Perry at Daystar TV.

My daughter, Angela, and granddaughter, Bethany taught me things about the computer too. If they had not helped me, I would not be typing my book on my computer. I am very grateful for that.

Gloria, Linda and Danva we were a team, we had a dream, we did beam!

I have a beautiful, mirrored tray for my perfume bottles that Mrs. Gloria gave to me. It reminds me of her and her willingness to teach me and to make me her assistant. To me, it reflects her trust in me. There were many more employees she could have chosen, but she chose me, and I felt extremely honored.

Six years later, I retired to be with Claude. I am glad I did retire, because I had four years to spend with Claude. We were free to go wherever our fancy took us. I knew I would miss Daystar and all my coworkers. I felt very compelled though to be with Claude. Now I know that God spoke to me. God knew Claude would be going to heaven in four years.

Linda Williams, the night supervisor at Daystar, edited the budget and some teachings I put together. The prayer department would send a copy of my budget or my teaching to people who needed an example.

Arnie, Gloria, Linda, Tami, Claudanna, Danva, Howard at Daystar.

Linda's daughter, Tami Watson, and my daughter, Claudanna, have been best friends for years, and now Linda and I are. It was neat to share an office with Linda and with Hugo Bacarreza. We all became good friends. We enjoyed our office, which had full-view windows. I think we had the best office in the whole building.

Claude would come and see me in our office sometimes, and we all would have a nice visit.

The Daystar Prayer Partners we are praying over the prayer requests.

Hugo gave me lessons in Spanish and bought me a Spanish-English dictionary. He also gave me a beautiful yellow vase with roses on it. I keep it in my kitchen because it matches the decor. I think of him when I look at that vase, and as I look at all the things people have given to me, I am touched. The vase reminds me of the roses Claude would give me.

Margaret Canafax, my friend from Daystar Television, gave me a small praying rabbit that holds his hand together, as well as a bird stand that says, "God's blessings surround us."

She also gave me a pretty, stuffed redbird. And she gave me a bird plant holder that says, "Bloom Where God Plants You." These are all reminders to hold onto God. She remembered the things that are close to my heart. What a close and wonderful friend she is!

Patricia Lee, a friend from Daystar, gave me a ceramic piece with letters that spell "Faith." This piece has helped remind me that I can be successful being on my own by faith. I wanted her to know that it has blessed me more than she will ever know. In my times of missing Claude, I would look at her gift and say, "I can walk by faith, each step I take."

I have another ceramic faith piece that I put in front of my fireplace that Claude Jr., Melanie, and Tessa gave to me. When I walk by it, I say, "Yes, I can make it through my journey by faith. God still has a plan for me, and now I am writing a book."

When I worked at Daystar, I had the honor of leading a girl by the name of Stacy Gunderson to Jesus. She was a new employee and would come into the prayer department for prayer. One day she came to me and said, "I have some problems. Will you pray with me?" I said, "Yes, I will."

I prayed with her, and then I had the urge to ask her if she had ever asked Jesus into her heart. She said she had not, so I led her in the sinner's prayer and she asked Jesus into her heart. What a wonderful moment that was! Her whole countenance changed.

We became good friends after that, and we did things together at Daystar.

One day, walking through the hall at Daystar, we saw each other. She had on a beautiful blue cross necklace with matching earrings. I told her how pretty they were and I made a joke that they were meant for me and not her. I never thought anymore about it. The jewelry brightened up her face and she looked lovely.

When I was retiring from Daystar, on the day I was to leave, Stacy gave me a white box. I opened it up and, to my astonishment inside were that beautiful blue cross necklace and the earrings. I was very touched.

I said, "I can't take your pretty jewelry!" She said, "You have to take it, because God told me to give it to you."

I gratefully accepted her gift and was so blessed by it. I would call her sometimes and tell her where I wore it and for what occasion.

One day when I was talking to someone on the phone, they told me Stacy had died giving birth to her baby. I was so crushed and heartbroken, but the Lord reminded me she was in heaven and that I had a part in her making it there. I then had to rejoice for her going home to heaven, as I have done with Claude's going to heaven.

I honor you, Stacy, by writing these words about you, and I love you. I will see you in heaven, my giving friend. You gave up something you treasured to bless someone like me.

Margie Young, a friend from Daystar, had someone make me a beautiful sun-catcher for my kitchen window. It has a white dove, representing the Holy Spirit, and the colors blue and yellow, which coordinate with my kitchen. It is a very stunning piece. I enjoy it very much in my window, and I have Margie to thank for that.

Margie also gave me a bird in a glass case on a stand that lights up. She remembered I liked birds too.

Knowing that I have a fur coat, she gave me a teddy bear from her collection. "This one is especially for you," she said. It has a real fur collar, and I think it is adorable. She really blessed me. When she left Daystar, I never saw her anymore. Margie, wherever you are, I enjoy the precious things that you have given to me. Every day I look at my sun-catcher and it reminds me I have the Holy Spirit with me.

Frankie Casey, a friend I worked with at two television stations—Success in Life and Daystar—knew I loved to dance. She gave me a precious cup from the "Sweet Me Collection Stoneware." On the cup it says, "The Sweetest Dancing Star" and it has a little girl dancing on it.

It thrills me when people remember what I enjoy in life. Working with her both times was a blessing to me. The cup reminds me to keep on dancing, and I will have joy when I am missing Claude.

Sharon Kerns, a friend from Daystar, gave me an unusual piece of art with six ducks and a blue heart in the middle. It is made with screen and framed with boards. She knew I collected ducks, so she gave it to me. Sharon went to heaven last year, and I was with her at her home when she was promoted.

Sharon was always giving me music CDs and good teachings. My favorite CD is Chuck Girard's *Voice of the Wind.* It reminds me that God is with me in the loss of Claude. I will see you in heaven, Sharon, my friend. You gave me one of your favorite art pieces. How it stirs my heart each time I look at it!

Betty Sanders, a friend from Daystar, gave me a set of beautiful blue and black earrings. I had commented to her about how pretty they were. One day, she put them in my hand and said, "I want you to have these and I want you to enjoy them." I felt such a sense of love from her when she did this. Betty and I used to say I was her teacher and she was my pet. Out of all the employees, she wanted to be my pet. We enjoyed our time to talk together.

Betty has since gone to heaven. She was a happy person, and I know my pet is enjoying her new home.

As you see, a lot of my friends have already met their Maker, and they were young people. I encourage people who read my book to be sure when their assignment is finished on earth that they are ready to go to heaven. I will see you, my friend Betty, in heaven. We will talk again there.

I met Wanda Salazar and her daughter, Laura Jane Gross, through the radio program where I worked. Wanda knew I collected ducks and said I could have a set of her duck dishes, glasses, silverware, and duck figurines.

I have ducks for the inside of my house and outside, thanks to my precious friend Wanda. I really enjoy the collection she gave me, and so did Claude. Bless you, Wanda, for thinking of us.

Roland and Eddie Lou Rhine, friends of mine and Claude's, gave us a Rose Maruri Masterpiece set of vases for our twenty-fifth wedding anniversary. I still am blessed when I walk by the shelf they are on.

We have had them for years, but the sight of them still portrays their beauty and reminds me that they took time to choose a special gift for us. The vases have added an excellent touch to our home. They help me embrace the memory of our marriage.

Timmy Eckhart, my nephew, painted a sixteen-by-twenty-inch oil portrait of me, and he did an excellent job. He wanted to do more of me, but I told him I have too many pictures of myself already. Claude always wanted large pictures of me. The work and the thought Timmy put into that painting were so sweet though. I wanted to acknowledge his work, because it was so nice of him to think of me.

Jerry Eckhart, Timmy's father, has done paintings for us too. My favorite is the eagle that he painted for us. As you know, I like eagles.

As I have shared with you some of the things people have blessed me with, I hope it has touched you as these memories have touched me. These people reached out to me and made a lasting impression upon me with their love. Their love has been such a comfort since the loss of Claude. All of the people and the things they have given to us now grace our home.

I realize the fog has lifted and the sun is shining brightly once again for me. All these memories shine like stars in my world and have been a part of the healing journey that I have held onto.

I thank everyone who has placed a part of his or her life into mine. God has seen your kind accomplishments to bless me. I pray that God will give to all of you many times over for what you have done for me.

Chapter Fourteen

GOD CONTROLS MY DESTINY

I F THERE IS ANYTHING BETTER THAN to be loved, it is to love in return. I learned, in my past relationships, what it is that makes a marriage work. I had the trust and sense of security that comes from a loving commitment and I know the value of communication and the warmth of deep and honest sharing.

We continued to love each other as time went by. These are some of the things that made my marriages so wonderful, and that is why I now have a foundation with rules of conduct to guide my future.

These rules apply to any relationship and aren't just for married couples.

I have been dating Howard Meister. He is the wonderful man who came to my rescue so many times to help me at my house. He had asked me out to eat many times, but I usually said, "I am just not ready to go out."

I have shared, in another chapter, how Howard installed a change-over switch for my generator. At the time, my son Claude Jr. and I had asked Howard to come over and give us a bid for doing this work. But then my son decided he wanted his friend to do it. He thought his friend could do it within one day, and he knew Howard would have to do a little bit every day when he got off work.

Howard has just reminded me of that day and how God spoke to him about me. He said, "It was the seventh day of February. The year was 2010 that you, my friend Danva, came to me at church. You asked me,

'Howard, do you know how to connect a change-over switch?' I said, 'I sure do know how, but please let me take a look at it. I would like to see what all would be involved.'"

Howard told me later that our conversation had been a mixture of pleasure and business for him.

I started talking to Howard the day he came over to give us a bid and said, "My birthday is this month on the twenty-fifth of February." I told him not once but three times while he was at my house. I know now the Holy Spirit was encouraging me to share my birthday.

Howard later told me, "When I left your house, I was very impressed to buy a birthday card for you. But knowing you had been widowed, I thought it would not be proper to do that. Still, the thought of buying you a card just kept coming to me and I could not think about anything else.

"The Holy Spirit told me, 'You go now and buy her the card.' I went to purchase you a card, but again I decided it wouldn't look very good for me to send you a card, since you had been widowed. I changed my mind. But then, the next day I said, 'So what I am going to anyway? Danva is my friend, and I am going to get her a card!'

"That evening, I talked myself out of it once more. Now it was the evening before your birthday, and my idea about sending you a birthday card would not stop. I finally decided to send you a card and to believe it would be received in friendship.

"I got into my car to go buy your card, but when I got to the Hallmark store, I found it was closed. I said, 'Now what I am going to do?' But then I thought, *Oh, grocery stores and drugstores have cards too!* The drugstore was the first one I came to.

"I always like to send a card with a biblical message. The first card I looked at was nice, but the second card had a perfect message for you, Danva. I held it in my hand and began to pick up another card. As I did, I heard the Holy Spirit say, 'The one in your hand is the card for Danva.' I quickly put the other card back and went and paid for the right one.

"I had brought stamps with me so I could mail your card that evening. I wanted it to arrive the next day, on your birthday. I addressed and stamped the envelope, and dropped the card in the Post Office box.

"Then I looked up to see the mail pickup time, and my excitement and my feelings sank in despair. I realized the pickup time was only once a day, at four p.m. Needless to say, the card didn't arrive on your birthday."

"You got the card the day after your birthday. You called me and told me it had blessed you so much. You wanted to let me know how much the message in it ministered to you. What a relief it was to know the card was received in friendship!"

I was so blessed by that card, and hearing about all the effort Howard made to get it to me was astounding. His graciousness would not go in vain, because God says if you bless the widow, you will be blessed too.

Claude Jr.'s friend lived out of state and he never was able to come to Texas to install that change-over switch. After five months passed, I called Howard back and ask him, "Do you still want to do the job?" and he said he did.

Howard and the transfer switch he installed for me and he did a great job!

Howard started coming over after work and installing the switch. He did an excellent job, as I have shared in my book. I don't think anyone could have done a better job.

Then one day, I had been working long hours on my book and I decided I needed to get out of the house for a while. I called Howard and said, "I am ready to go out with you to eat, if the offer is still on."

Howard said, "Yes, it is. And would you like to go to church too?"

I agreed, and we had a very enjoyable evening. I hadn't talked so much to anyone in a long time.

Our conversation became a special new time for me. I felt I could really communicate with Howard. It was a heaven-born relationship with enjoyable possibilities of future times together.

Howard and I learned a lot about each other that evening. Each of us was the third oldest child in our families. We were both born in the same month—Howard was born on the twelfth of February and I was born on the twenty-fifth. Both of us were born in the year 1945. We both came from large families; there were eight children in my family and seventeen in Howard's!

We both like to teach the Word of God and lead others to Jesus. We both have done bus ministries at churches.

As the evening went on, I asked Howard, "Did you ever know Kenneth Hagin?"

He said, "Yes, I did. I went to his Bible school in Broken Arrow, Oklahoma."

I replied, "That is wonderful that you have gone to Rhema Bible Training Center. My life changed so much, thirty years ago, when I started listening to Kenneth Hagin's teachings. Here we have something more in common."

Howard said, "Yes, we do have a lot in common."

We continued to date. But then, one day, I felt I needed to do a sabbatical. I wanted to hear from God what He wanted me to write in my book. I told Howard, "I need to be alone so I can work on my book."

Howard replied, "Just call me when you are through and I will take you out to eat."

I said, "Thank you, Howard. I will look forward to that."

I had two months of seeking God and hearing his voice. I can say it was one of the most important set-apart times I've had with God. I really enjoyed hearing from God and being in His presence. My pastor, Floyd Ellsworth, approved and gave his blessing while I did my sabbatical.

Two months had passed since I had started my sabbatical and I had not talked with Howard. I decided to give him a call. I said, "Howard, I am ready to go out if you still want to."

He said, "Great! How about going out tonight?"

A storybook, precious love story began then, and God orchestrated all of it. It was like peace and righteousness kissed each other and blessed my relationship with Howard. This provided a new lease on life for the both of us, which brought us both joy and contentment. I had never thought I would have someone to love me again.

The sky opened up to us like an archaic, elegant, old-fashioned mirror. It looked down at Howard and me and cast us into a mold. It was processing us to form our lives with each other. The sky mirror looked down at us and saw all we were doing, and God said, "I have a plan for these two. They will make a team for me. They will be heirs together, and they'll be cheerful and successful."

Howard and I have the victory to achieve a good relationship. God had a purpose in allowing us to start dating. It excites me to know He knows what is best for me and how great His plans will be!

God bestirred Himself for me and has made my dwelling in life prosperous. He opened the door to let me enjoy life with a wonderful, trusting person. Though the beginning of my life, the part with Claude had stopped, the next part of my life was greatly increased by knowing Howard.

For such a time as this, God allowed Howard to come into my life. God has restored my face with joy. In a special, designated moment, God allowed my heart to open to Howard. It was astounding and extra wonderful.

I had been storm tossed, but God stood by me, and He had my future planned. I can say He made all the walls of my life to become enclosed. He enclosed them with beautiful colors and sealed them with antimony to harden the walls to protect me.

I started to focus on edifying others and their needs instead of focusing on grief. I went to nursing homes, and Howard went with me. He would teach the people and build them up, and I would sing. Even though I was still hurting, this is the reason I am not still grieving. I could not be absorbed in my issues any longer.

Howard gave me a multitude of compassions from his heart. He became active on my behalf. I had not been eating well, and he would cook food for me every week and bring it to me. I can see now that God provided for me, the widow, through Howard.

God earnestly remembered me and used Howard to bless me. Howard's best deeds hurried to me and God's favor has come to the both of us. How beautiful and holy our relationship's started! It was very pleasant and desirable, and it still is.

Considering the calamities I have gone through, God sent Howard to come to my aid. As the juice of a grape which is found in the cluster has a blessing in it, that was how God gave him to me. God destined us to be together, and we are the blessed of the Lord.

My widow's life was not all sadness anymore. It was rising out of the depths of loss, and I was beginning new growth. I centered my attention on a clear image of myself and my future. My mourning had exhausted itself.

I then asked God, "What's next? Will you show me your wisdom and why I am left alone?"

God showed me. Wisdom starts with listening. I started searching for it, and God became the source of my wisdom. This gave me a symbol of peace to enhance my life.

My search brought to me the brilliance of security with Howard, because of his smiling face and excellent attitude and all the things he did for me. He did not charge me anything for his repair services, because I was a widow. God has given a jewel to me, a man whom I did not even have to go looking for. God just put him in my path. I encourage anyone who is lonely to let God order your steps.

People have told me they see that the hand of the Lord has put Howard in my life. God excites me with His plan for us.

Our hearts were joined by heaven's kiss. Julia Bright created this picture.

I will never forget the first time Howard kissed me. I can tell you, I heard the sound of bells in my head. I felt like I had never been kissed before. This kiss was like your first love, so tender and innocent. There was nothing ugly or sinful about it. I can say I have never been kissed by anyone with that kind of intensity or energy before. I realized this kiss was made in heaven.

You know what? I have to tell you, it still happens when Howard kisses me. It is energy from heaven that God gave to Howard and me. We tapped into the way God wants true love to be. I think Adam and Eve probably experienced this too, and when they sinned it was lost. They no longer were able to hold onto the kiss from heaven.

I want to encourage all singles to stay pure. You can then have the pureness of your relationships with the one you date. That ultimate affection will come down from heaven and embrace each of you.

You will experience a highly enjoyable, expressive kiss for each other. It will be totally made in heaven. God only allows this kiss from the one He has chosen for you. God put us together, and we did not plan our destiny.

American Airlines has called Howard back to Oklahoma to work. He had been laid off seven years ago. He had asked me to agree in prayer with him, a few months earlier, that the airline would call him back. We even made a written petition to God for this to come about. We prayed about it, and God heard our prayers.

Howard was so excited when he told me he'd been called back to work! He said, "I will have to go to Tulsa and work for an extended time and then put in for a transfer to Texas. There is one thing, though. I'll have to live there for a while."

I felt a numbness coming over me when I realized I would not have Howard to do things with. I had enjoyed our dates and times together very much.

Change has to come in our lives though, for us to go to the next level.

I looked at Howard with tears in my eyes, and I noticed he had something behind his back. He proceeded to go get a kitchen barstool and placed it in the middle of my living room floor. Then he asked me to sit on the stool.

To my surprise, he laid around my feet three beautiful bouquets of flowers. The next thing I heard was Howard saying, "I don't want to go alone, and I don't want you to be alone in Texas by yourself. Danva, will you marry me and go with me?"

Howard picked up the flowers and gave them to me. Holding all my three bouquets of flowers, I quickly said, "Yes."

This was another remarkable occurrence of God using the number three in my life, and I love it. I knew God had orchestrated it all. I was aroused to excitement and a stirring of my spirit.

I had never thought I would marry again or even have someone to love for a third time.

I would not be by myself anymore. God's timing for this was perfect. God put my life in order and helped me see that He had sent Howard to me and me to Howard.

God was giving me my third husband. Wow! I am impressed with God. He sure knows how to order my steps!

I have learned our lives are planned for us by God. I can now tell everyone, "Enjoy your journey in life. No matter what you go through, everything is going to come out all right."

I did not plan this time of my life, but there is someone who did. May I introduce you to him? His name is Jesus, and He is my best friend. He hangs out the stars and tells the sun to shine. He kisses the flowers each morning with dew, but He's not too busy to care about you.

I called Claudanna to tell her Howard had asked me to marry him. She said, "Mom, Dad came to me last night in a dream. He said, 'Claudanna, Howard is going to be your new dad and a husband to your mom. He will be a good husband and dad.'"

Like an angel sent down from heaven, our precious Claude gave his blessing and approval. It was a confirmation to us because God used a dream to say we were in His will. God does speak in dreams, visions, and sometimes in a still, small voice. Some may say they don't believe that, but God does things that are supernatural.

Job 33:14–15 (AMP) says, "For God does reveal His will. He speaks not only once but more than once. One may hear God's voice in a dream, or a vision of the night when deep sleep falls on them."

Howard knows I loved Claude and he loved him too, because he was Claude's friend. Howard does not mind at all. I will always love him, because of the great husband and dad he was. Out of respect for Claude, I wanted to make sure for a year that I had properly honored him.

Bethany, my granddaughter, told me, "Nana, if you had married the next day, God would not care. God did not put a time limit on it—the world did." And I agree with her.

I am going through another chapter in my life though, beginning with Howard. No one can take Claude's place, and no one can take Howard's place either. Both Claude and Howard are their own special kind of person in my life. For this particular season in my life, which God planned before

I was born, God has given me love once more. How sweet and precious it is!

I don't have to be alone anymore, and God directs my steps. He has just given me another man to love. I feel honored to have been married to three wonderful men!

Job 33:29 says, "Behold, God does all these things twice, yes, three times." In the same way, he has given me three husbands to love.

Bethany called me and gave me a Scripture. She said, "Nana, in Romans 7:2–3 (AMP), it says a married woman is bound by law to her husband as long as he lives, but if her husband dies, she is loosed and discharged from the law concerning her husband. When her husband dies, the marriage law no longer is binding on her. She is free from the law. Nana, you are doing nothing wrong by marrying Howard. You need to have someone to continue your life with."

Bethany's heart was for me to have peace in my life and to go on with my life. She loved her papa very much. She also loves me, so she reached out to me through the Word of God. How precious is the love, she showed to me.

I want my life and book to impact a person who desperately needs an encouraging word. Pleasant words are as a honeycomb, sweet to the soul, which is healing to us. I think that is a wonderful way to describe when we have a conversation with someone. It can be medicine to a weary soul and healing to a bruised spirit. Kind words, spoken in due season, are God's bridges of love.

I have the confidence of knowing I have been led by God and my steps have been ordered by him. I have always prayed for God to take me to my destiny, and He has. Howard and I have ministered together for our God. We will continue to do so, and that is why He put us together.

Howard, Danva, at our Wedding and picture taken by Nancy Southard.

We started planning our wedding, because soon we would be going to Tulsa. We thought we had only two weeks, but it ended up being two months. We needed that time to put our two houses together. We had a big job on our hands, and we gave a lot of things away.

We also had to decide what we were taking to Oklahoma with us. We did it though, and you should see our house. It blends both of our families. We want our children to feel they are all a part of us, so we added pictures of Howard's family to go with mine on the walls. Howard's things enhance our home.

Now I have to tell you about our fast-planned wedding. Claudanna, our daughter, helped us organize. She took care of the refreshments, our wedding cake, and my bouquet. We could not have made this happen without her. She has been a blessing to Howard and me from the first minute that she knew we were dating. I can say she is a beautiful person inside and out. Even though she is our daughter, she is a genuine precious jewel sent from heaven for such a time as this.

Lessie, a member of our church, made a wedding cake for us, and that was so sweet of her. We did not have time to invite everyone to our wedding. She did not even get invited to the wedding, and I honor her for having a servant's heart toward us. Both cakes were very yummy!

Howard, Danva and our grandchildren in our wedding, they are so cute.

We asked our smallest grandchildren to be in the wedding. Jaxson Hamilton was our ring-bearer, and Joscelyn Hamilton, Andrea Sanner, Aylisa Anthony, and Tessa York were our flower girls.

The girls said, "Nana, we don't have any flowers to carry!"

I said, "I will ask Pastor Michelle if I can borrow some of the flowers in the vases at church." I asked her, and she agreed. She was so sweet to assist me.

I also had to come up with something for Jaxson to carry the wedding rings in. I found a pretty bowl, and that served our need. The children looked absolutely adorable. It could not have been any better if we'd had many rehearsals.

Howard, Danva and our children in our wedding and sweet they are.

Our children—Carla Hamilton, Claudanna Sanner, Anju Chettri, and Claude York Jr.—stood up with us as we were married. Mark Meister and Angela MacLeod were not able to attend.

"Our Blessed Blended Family" Mark, Carla, (Howard's children) Angela, Claudanna, Claude Jr., Anju (my children) we are now a blended family and I love them all more than they will ever know.

Howard and I have beautiful children and grandchildren. Now we both have gained some more jewels in our lives.

Mark Meister, Howard's son.

Howard, Betty, Kristin, Mark, Sky, Elizabeth. They are my precious extended family that I love.

Mark lives in Oklahoma with his wife Kristin, daughter Elizabeth, our granddaughter. In this picture is Kristin's parents Sky and Betty Sharp.

Carla Meister Hamilton, Howard's daughter and her children. Joscelyn his granddaughter and Jaxson his grandson. They are my precious extended family that I love.

Howard, Danva, Carla, Joscelyn and Jaxson at Mark's house.

Pastor Floyd Ellsworth planned an excellent ceremony for us, and we appreciate his love and agreement to bless our marriage. He believed God put us together and he touched our hearts.

Darrell and Barbara Decker prayed a wonderful prayer over us. As we knelt down, Barbara held a Jewish prayer shawl over our heads.

Then we stood before the man of God, our Pastor Floyd, to marry us. All of our children and grandchildren who could be there stood with us too.

My sister Nancy, her husband Kenny Southard, and my sister Charlotte Yeathermon captured the event with great photographs. To see all the children and grandchildren looking on, it was such a sweet scene. I would not take anything for those pictures. We appreciate Nancy, Kenny, and Charlotte's gift to us.

Oscar Dale, Charlotte, Kenny, & Nancy at our wedding Ah! I love them!

Kenny and Nancy made a great DVD of the wedding with background music. They put together a beautiful wedding photo album with the pictures they took at our wedding. That was a nice blessing for us. I say to Kenny, Nancy, and Charlotte, "Thank you all, and you did a most remarkable job!"

We plan to do a renewal of our vows when we can invite everyone. I have to say though that this wedding was picture perfect, and everyone there had a part in it.

I love it when the Holy Spirit takes charge and everything just turns out to be wonderful. It was a storybook wedding made with Jesus and our angels standing with us. I know they were cheering us on and saying, "This is the day the Lord has made! Rejoice and be glad in it."

We have gotten an opportunity that many do not get. Howard and I are very honored and grateful that God chose to put us together.

We want all of our children to call us Dad and Mom and our grandchildren to call us Paw Paw and Nana, when they want to.

Howard and I are happy. Our marriage was made in heaven and the proof is in our pictures and faces.

When our friend, Carrie Rivers, heard that we had gotten married, she said, "Praise God! There is hope for me and all the singles for God to give us husbands!"

There is a very important part in Howard's life that I would like to share. Howard had not been married for twenty-three years. He had told God, "I am not marrying again until You bring me the right one."

These are the five things God told Howard to look for in a wife. God told him, "These things will let you know that this is the wife for you."

1. She would be connected to heaven with a salvation experience.
2. She would be filled with the Holy Spirit and speak in tongues.
3. She would be a woman of prayer.
4. She would have an evangelist anointing and pray for people to get saved.
5. She would desire to teach the Word of God.

Howard told God, "I want that very much in my wife. And God, I have three requests that I would like my wife to have."

1. I want a wife with all the things you said she would have (1–5).
2. I want a wife with energy who wants to go and do things and not just sit around.
3. I want a wife who wants to please heaven.

Instead of my former grief, I now have a twofold recompense to rejoice. Some people have said that Howard and I are people the Lord has blessed. We greatly rejoice in the Lord for that. He has covered us with His robe of righteousness.

Howard and I holding hands, posing after our wedding, we still hold hands.

God prepared Howard, the bridegroom, for me. He adorned me, the bride, with cheerfulness. I have a sparkle in my eye and the vivid desire to be a virtuous woman, which God and Howard had decreed I would be.

We both had no idea we would marry until God established our steps. We did not have to look for a mate. God sought us, and He made the plan.

We look forward to our future. Neither of us is alone anymore. I can say God does care about the singles. He wants us to have a twofold unity, protected by Him.

Sometimes, people comment that our faces shine even in the pictures they see of Howard and me. It has to be the radiance of the glory of the Lord that has risen upon us and is seen on us.

Our family has enlarged, and we both want to gather them in our arms and love them all equally. Everyone shall be a joy to each other from age to age.

Howard and I have appointed love, peace, and righteousness as our taskmasters. The Lord Jesus shall be the everlasting light of our new family. One by one, they will find their place with us and accept God's plan that put Howard and me together. We shall become a strong family. The Lord Jesus has hastened us to this appointed time in our lives.

We have entered into the treasures of life, where light dwells and distributes to us and satisfies the longing to be loved another time. This light does not dwell in a place but dwells in us. There is a channel for torrents of rain and clusters of stars shining down on us. This makes a clear path for our lives together.

We have climbed safely to a mountain and, like eagles do, we are now swift to mount up at God's command and to stretch our lives to His plan. We both want our lives to have dignity, wisdom, and excellence. We want to array ourselves with integrity and honesty, and we want our appearance to wave the plumage of our love.

We are growing in grace and we are full of sap, with spiritual and physical vitality.

We want to bring forth in our love good fruit. As we study God's Word together, we will flourish. We want to be living memorials to show the Lord Jesus is the rock in our lives and our marriage.

We are staying at a hotel suite in Tulsa, where Howard's job sent him. I was privileged to pray with ten employees at the hotel suite where we are staying. I would go down in the mornings to get coffee and God would put people in my path.

I started talking to them and we just became friends. I shared with them about Jesus.

I asked them, "If you were to die tonight, do you know for sure you would go to heaven?"

"They replied, "No, I do not know."

I asked them, "May I pray with you to ask Jesus into your heart? All ten of them wanted to pray with me, and they accepted Jesus in their hearts!" Some of them were Spanish and I had to have an interpreter.

Howard and I decided to buy them Bibles in Spanish. How exciting it was to watch their faces light up when we gave them the Bibles.

Howard led a man to the Lord at a gas station when we were leaving from Texas to come to Tulsa. This man came over to our car while Howard was cleaning our windows. The man asked, "Can I clean off your windows for you? I need money for gas."

Howard let him talk a while then we both knew he needed Jesus. Then Howard told him, "You don't have to clean my windows, but I will buy you some gas."

Then Howard asked him, "Can I pray with you?" The man said, "Yes." Howard prayed and then asked me to pray too. He accepted Jesus into his heart. We told him where to find our church, Oasis Community Worship Center. We encouraged him to go to church.

In both Howard and me, God has put a desire to win souls to Jesus. We make a good team, and I am going to name us the soul-winner writers.

Another incident happened when we were leaving the hotel today. We were packing the car to come back to Texas. Suddenly a man and woman drove up. The man called out to Howard, "Hey, I have to go out of town. My father has died and I need gas money to go to Arkansas. Can you spare any money to help me, please?"

Howard reached in his pocket and gave him some money to help him.

Then I felt to go over to the couple and pray with them. They both prayed with me and asked Jesus into their hearts. I think Howard and I are a team, and God sure knows how to put people in our path. I say, "I think we were on an assignment today, from God."

When we get in line with God's will for our lives and yield to the things He has put in us, then our path will become clearer every day.

Whatever He has for us to do for him, we will know it. Then we will be in the perfect will of God for our lives.

As Howard and I have yielded to the assignment of God for us today, this became a purpose for us. It is fulfilling to find out the purpose that God created us for and get to see it unfold in our lives.

No man or woman can come between us, because God has joined us together, and we shall look forward to our future. Especially when we get to minister together and see people get saved. Our marriage was arranged by heaven. Through Claudanna's dream, Claude gave the mantle of being my husband to Howard. This mantle is a covering to protect me and stand by my side throughout the rest of my life and in our ministry.

Howard and I both take marriage as a vow to be kept and never broken. We will keep our vow to God and serve him. We also want to be in God's perfect will and always yield to his assignments.

I would like to share that Howard came from a family of seventeen children. His parents, Edward and Pearl Meister never divorced. I came from a family of eight children and my parents, Oscar and Dorothy Curington never divorced either. We both know the value of having a family.

I have pictures of my brother and sisters I have shared in my book. Now I want to share here Howard's brothers and sisters. His family was larger than mine, but that means more memories to share, more love to give. I know they all have happy stories to tell.

Here are Howard's twelve brothers and five sisters. Back to front: Everett, Howard, Willie, Harold, Les, Eli, Phillip, Ernie, Dan, George, Ben, Mike, Lucy, Arlene, Anna, Alma and Martha. They represent a strong loving family.

Karen Meister (Danny's wife) and Kathy Meister (Everett wife) sent me the family pictures. They were a blessing to me and I so wanted to have the Meister family picture in my book.

I have only talked to Karen over the phone and through e-mail. I met Kathy one time but I can say they are family to me. They have added a special touch to my book. I talked about getting to know people in my book and you need fellowship for that to happen. This is a great example. I look forward one day going to Fairbury, Illinois to meet all of the Meister family.

*This is a fun picture of the Meister seventeen children and their
mates. They all have their backs in the picture to show their place
in the family. How unique this picture is and I love it, love it!*

My sweet husband is the third child in his family and I am the third child
in my family too. Do you remember how God uses the number three in
my life? This makes it is very symbolic to me.

People say, "I am proud to be an American and I am." I am proud to
be a Meister too.

Life is full of great surprises. I have learned no matter what happens
God will work everything out for my good.

Chapter Fifteen

DREAMS FROM HEAVEN

DREAM NUMBER ONE: JUNE 9, 2011

I HAD A DREAM AND AN ENCOUNTER from heaven, which was a sign of jubilant exaltation. I was in my hotel suite in Tulsa, Oklahoma. I began to hear Claude's voice in my spirit, although I could not see him. He said, "Even though I took care of you for forty-four years, now the mantle has been handed down to Howard. He will take good care of you and I have released you to him. This mantle has been a covering to protect you and it will always be with you."

Claude and Danva our love that is endless even in eternity.

I continued to hear Claude in my spirit. He said, "I know your needs and I don't want you to be alone. Howard is the one for you to go through the rest of your journey in life with. He will help you fulfill your destiny."

I felt total peace as he talked to me, and it was by the Spirit of God that I could hear his voice. It was only our spirits communicating, as God allowed it. I became more aware of the supernatural then than I had at any time of my life.

Claude said, "I will always love you and I am at peace in heaven. This releases peace to you, because God is not through with you. You needed a helpmate, and God planned for Howard to stand by your side in love and ministry. It will be a ministry that God has called both of you to do."

He kept speaking. "Thoughts of heaven are different than thoughts on earth. They blend for every situation. This includes your beautiful life, to have someone to love and take care of you. I was looking from heaven when you led those ten people to Jesus. I am so proud of you and always have been. My love for you will go on through eternity.

"You have now heard my voice in a different way. Just remember what Pastor Terri said—that you should talk to me just like you talk to Jesus.

"You have been released to be able to hear in your spirit and let me talk to you in the spirit. Remember I did not die. I just went to heaven.

"I pray for Howard and you and for our children and grandchildren. I am blessed to see you happy. We in heaven rejoice that you are happy! God has a plan for you, and Howard is part of that plan.

"Remember in heaven there is only love—no jealousy, no hate, no stress, no bad thoughts. So I release you, my precious Danva, to go on with your life with Howard by your side. He is a good husband for you. God set him aside for twenty-three years until he could marry you.

"It's all in God's plan. He knows what is best for you. You now have had three men to love you. We will all love you forever. You're the woman we would all marry all over again.

"Hold your head up, because God has your life in the palm of His hands. He knew you would write a book about your three husbands.

"You have tapped into heaven, where many people have not. It is a releasing of your spirit to hear through God's spirit. You see, no one's spirit dies—only our bodies die. We are alive forever in heaven, and it is exciting here. Someday, we can walk in heaven together.

"Tell Doug, Angela, Beth, Aylisa, Caleb, Austin, Jim, Claudanna, Lauren, Jeremy, Andrea, Claude Jr., Melanie, Tessa, Anju, and Wanda that I love them. As they all love each other, this will be them loving me too. I am a part of them, which is a stronger bond than on earth.

"God is love, and heaven only breathes love and forgiveness. Tell everyone to love each other. That is the key to life. No matter what anyone does to you, forgive them and love them, and you will open the door of a spiritual return of uniting our family with peace.

"Tell Howard I am honored that he accepted you as God's choice for him. I approve, and I am at peace because you are being taken care of so wonderfully!

"I will love you forever, Danva. I want you to blossom in your life with Howard."

Dream Number Two

I woke on July 1, 2011, in my home in Hurst and remembered an absolutely wonderful dream. I had been with Claude in a huge house. He took me through each room, and I was amazed at how big each room was.

I loved the pantry because it was a round room with shelves all around it. It was a woman's dream to be able to reach whatever she would need to get and not have to dig to find it.

As I walked through the house, I told Claude, "I wish our children were here with us in this beautiful, huge house."

Then we walked into the most spacious, marvelous kitchen I had ever seen. The kitchen island was laid out for a queen to work on. "My! My!" I said. "I could spend some enjoyable time making creative dishes on this kitchen island."

Then, to my astonishment, Claude showed me all the delicious-looking dishes he had made himself. I said, "I didn't know you knew how to make all this food."

He said, "I have learned how to, and I have enjoyed cooking and baking all of this."

When I turned toward the stove, it seemed as big as a room. I saw these sparkling biscuits Claude had made. They looked like there were tiny stars as they sparkled, and I could taste them in my mouth.

I had never seen Claude so happy before. He was in his habitat, and he was so enthused about everything in this house.

When I woke up from my dream, I pondered it. I said, "Oh, my goodness, I was in heaven in Claude's mansion!" I realized that was why the rooms were so big.

I was so blessed that God allowed me to see Claude and talk to him. It was wonderful to see him so content and happy.

As my daughter, Angela, reminded me, Claude always watched what he ate here on earth so he wouldn't get high cholesterol. He now can eat heaven's food, which is nothing anyone on earth can cook. Heaven is real, and I hope my book makes everyone realize that it is a heartbeat away.

God is a good God to let me step into heaven and see a part of Claude's life there. I am grateful knowing he is happy and content. I know the love he had for me. His releasing me to another man is a heaven decision that can only say I am loved.

I can say, "I'm an ordinary person who can write an extraordinary book because of Jesus in me. Wow, isn't God good?"

I made God my spiritual home when I unpacked my private feelings in writing this book. I made Him my reference point. His standards became the criteria for the way I live.

As I dealt with my life, I didn't use the world's standards to survive. I had to spend time with God and the Bible. I had to let my hair down and allow Him to speak to me and take one day at a time.

I believe this allowed me to have these dreams, to show me a side of His kingdom that otherwise I would not get to see. I feel honored to have had these dreams.

I have learned to hold fast to God, to stand still when I need to, and to be quiet before him. God has arranged all things for me because of His good will. He has purposes and plans and desires that reach far beyond my present view. I will rest with this thought and leave all else to Him.

My heart, mind, hands, voice, and feet—and my writing—are all stamped with the imprint of the Creator, my God. God is the larger context and plot in which my stories unfold.

The ability to see the big picture of my future is not based on my intellectual ability. It's based on getting and sharing God's wisdom. I want to always bask in the presence of God and do as He says. Then I know more exciting doors will open up to me. I will say to my precious heavenly Father, "Take me to my destiny."

God is looking at me in the spirit realm. I have experienced the power of it. I want to share an incident that happened to me after I had these dreams.

I was in the Sunflower Shop shopping and bent down to pick up a health bar that was in a basket. I noticed a lady bent down at the same time as I did. We both lifted up our heads at the same time. When I saw her face, lo and behold it was Dina Peller. She was my neighbor from a few years ago.

I said, "Hi Dina," and she replied, "Hi Danva." We began talking, and I shared with her my dreams I had recently had. She said, "Danva, I can see in your face and eyes you have had a visit to heaven. This excited me because it was such a confirmation my dreams were from heaven.

I love Isaiah 11:2. The first part of the Scripture applied to what went on in my dream. The Spirit of the Lord did rest upon me, the spirit of wisdom and understanding. This happened to me through these dreams.

God knew it was important enough to me so He sent Claude to speak to me in dreams.

I remembered the Scriptures in Job 33:15, 23 and I realized they applied to me. One may hear God's voice in a dream. For the hearer, which happened to be me, it included a messenger or an angel to show (me) what is right (for me) and that God has His hand on my life.

Chapter Sixteen

THREE WONDERFUL MEN

Eddie Williams my first husband a great man.

Claude Ray York Sr. my second husband a great man.

Howard Meister my third husband a great man.

Eddie, Claude, and Howard have provided color and spice to my life. They are all heroes of great courage and nobility to me. My life would have been, and would be, very boring without them. Their presence in my life has created a beautiful boutique of love, which I have felt and feel from all of them.

To have three wonderful men to love me is beyond the normal. There are women who have never had one husband. I have been honored by God to have three.

It is not that I am so worthy, but it is because of God's grace and mercy. I don't take it for granted. I love them all, but each in a different way. Each one had his own special part in my life.

I call all three of them "My Angel Army" who loved me and love me, just like Howard loves me now. I can admire them. They are the symbols of living life itself. This is what it means to be human, because they have involved themselves deeply with me.

I want my stories to tell people how, in fact, I did live and did survive. I authenticated the reality of our lives together. God used Eddie and Claude, and now Howard, to work out His purpose for my life.

God provides both plot and texture to every day of my life. This cluster of interlocking stories trained me in my perception of myself. I know I am not the leading character in my life. God gave me a place in His story.

God ordered my steps before I was even in my mother's womb. No one can deny that God gave me all three men. I am a very blessed woman to have shared a part of my life with each one of them.

Howard has taken center stage now in my life. He is the husband for me to continue my journey with. He is so easygoing and such a good conversationalist and his love for me can only be described as genuine. Our life is full of fun and laughter. I can say, "I am very happy to have Howard, and he lights up my life."

The blessings of God are upon Howard and me. An embellishment of alertness and delightful activity has blossomed in our marriage. A symbol of peace is within each of us. We have received a quality, exciting bond of unity. This has produced an affectionate, tender love we had never experienced before.

Howard was sanctified, purified, and set aside for me for twenty-three years. He has been brought to me by a connection from heaven. Do you know who that connection was? It was God Almighty Himself. What a well-preserved, loving husband He gave to me.

I thought no one could ever love me like Claude. *You know, no one can, and that's all right because Howard loves me too, but in his own way.* God put Howard and me together and our love is unique.

All of my husbands have been different, but they are all God's creation. They all have had different personalities, careers, hobbies, and interests. They all have loved me in their own way. This leaves no room for comparing any of my husband's because they are unique men.

Oh, my goodness! To my amazement, I adapted to all of them. We each blended. How could I not adapt? I had three outstanding men.

I am going to live for my future now and not live in the past, even though my past was good. I have to let it go and live in my today and tomorrow with Howard.

This is a new beginning for me, and I am excited. I do thank God for the three men of my life. God says in His Word, in Philippians 3:13 (TLB), that we should forget the past and look forward to what lies ahead.

I intend to do that with Howard.

Howard has graciously helped me edit my book. We have spent many hours together working on it. He has a knack for spotting things to improve anything he works on.

I watched him feel the parts; tears came to his eyes as he read parts of the book. He has read out loud my whole book as we edited it.

I have a gold mine with Howard and I don't know anything that he cannot do. He amazes me every day because of the wisdom he has. His job at American Airlines requires wisdom, and people's lives are in his hands with the job he does. He has to be alert and have wisdom for it.

I looked on the Internet to see what the job description for an editor and a book publisher was. Howard fits the description very well. The book publisher has to work well with deadlines and have strong communication skills. He or she must be a quick analytical reader, and he is.

I see our future together writing books and preparing teachings we both have. It will be an asset to have someone who is analytical to help me with my writing. See, God knew what He was doing when he put us together. Soul-winner writers we will be. I say, "It is fun, fun, fun, to live with Howard!"

I can say, "Our teamwork will make our dreams work. God knows our thoughts, desires, purposes, and endeavors. He will bless what Howard and I put our hands to, in the name of Jesus."

I can say, "My husband Howard is a number one master crafter and a number one man God chose for me."

Chapter Seventeen

MY SUGGESTIONS OF THINGS TO DO FOR YOURSELF

IRST, I SUGGEST THAT YOU REMIND yourself that this time of grief serves a purpose. God created us with an inherent, natural ability to heal. Our grief process is designed to bless us with healing, which I have experienced. It is in those hard moments that you need to take your grief by the neck and shout, "I will not let go until you bless me!" I agree with this quote from Pastor George Pearsons: "You have to refuse the pressure and stress and choose instead to enter the rest."

Second, everyone should know where their important papers are kept. I have three fireboxes where I keep my significant information. I have categorized these files and in front of each box I have written a list of its contents. I wanted to make it easy for whoever needed to find the files. I had also shown my system to Claude, my children, and now Howard.

Third, I believe everyone needs to be on a budget. I am so glad I knew how to manage our finances. I showed many families how to budget their income when I worked at Daystar Television. I developed a budget that Daystar used for people who called in for prayer concerning their finances.

I had to revise my own budget when Claude went to heaven, because my income changed. When you give the tithe to God from the gross amount, God will always help you use the balance wisely. God does that for me and I know He will do that for you. The budget template I developed is at the end of the book.

If your spouse was receiving retirement and Social Security checks, you will need to notify both his former employer and the Social Security office. If your spouse was still working, you will need to notify his or her employer. I suggest that you put enough money into a savings account to live on for two or three months.

Claude had already received his retirement and Social Security checks for the month when he was promoted to heaven. I had to return both checks and live on what I had in the bank and what my grandson Austin gave me. God bless Austin! He really helped me with the gift of his savings.

It took about three months of red tape for me to start receiving my portion of the checks I had returned. When I received the checks I had returned and the life insurance money, I paid my tithe off the gross amount, and I was also able to pay off a pledge that we had made. I know God intervened for me because, when I finally started receiving my checks regularly, they were more than I thought they would be. I praise God for that blessing.

I think it is very important to prepay the cost of your funeral if you can, so your loved ones will not have that to contend with. My mother went to heaven four years before Claude. With the money I received from her estate and some of my savings, I prepaid our funeral expenses.

We had purchased our cemetery plots twenty years earlier, and we got them at a very good price. In four years, the funeral expense had doubled in price.

I would suggest that the purchase of the funeral and the plot be done when you are young, if that is possible, because they cannot increase the price after you have bought them.

If you don't have the cash to buy them outright, terms can be arranged. If someone does pass, then the policy you purchased would defray the expense.

I never dreamed I was doing it for me, but it did become easier knowing we had made most of the decisions some time before Claude's death and our funerals were already paid for.

You will need to purchase death certificates. I suggest you buy at least twenty, because at most places one will be required. My lawyer told me it is against the law to make copies.

You will need to send a death certificate to your insurance companies, the Social Security office, your pension plan, utilities offices, burglar alarm system provider, banks, and your lawyer. If you sell or trade your car, a death certificate is required if the title is not in your name.

I ordered twenty because they are cheaper if you buy more than a few. You will be surprised at how many businesses require a death certificate.

The funeral home requires a death certificate also. You buy the certificates right there at the funeral home.

You will need to go to your bank and have your regular account, savings account, and any other transactions that the bank takes care of for you changed into your name. We had already made our children beneficiaries at our bank, so they would not have to wait until the will was probated. If you have not done that, this would be a good time to take care of it.

In some states, you will need to close savings and checking accounts that are in your spouse's name before they are frozen, pending the settlement of the estate.

I am so blessed to bank at Chase Bank in Hurst, Texas. I feel that the people there are my friends. Miki Hawkins helped me with all my business during the time I was experiencing such stress after losing Claude. She was like an angel on assignment for me. She went beyond her call of duty.

Zachary Tubb encouraged me and gave me a CD called *Are You Ready for the Rapture?* from his church. It was about the men in heaven that God was training to come back to earth and win people to Jesus. We both agreed Claude would be one of those to come back and work with Jesus in His return to the earth after the tribulation.

Miki and Zachary taught me how to pay my bills online, and it so easy to do now. They were good teachers.

Catherine Uberman, Shelly Green, Jared Lancon, Beth McLeod, and Joanna Rivera were such a comfort and help to me, and they all loved Claude and miss him too.

We had a life insurance policy, and I used the money I received from that to buy a new car. I recommend any widow do this so that you will have a reliable source of transportation and peace of mind knowing that the car is not going to give you any problems. Most of the time, you will be driving alone. Having a good car provides security.

The remainder of the money I invested in Franklin Templeton Investments. I had a wonderful man of God, Steve Wisdom, CFP, from Cosmoline Financial, who advised me where to invest. Steve also gave me advice about which car to buy, based on his experience. I took his advice because he had helped Claude invest his stock when Claude retired from Bell Helicopter. When I retired from Daystar, Steve helped me decide where to invest my retirement. I knew he could be trusted and was a man of integrity.

Claude and I met Steve through his uncle, Don Spears, a Christian financial advisor who had a radio program. We had also gone to the same church in the past. We had attended many classes on how to manage your finances, which Don held at our church.

We called Don to help us with investing Claude's stock, and he sent Steve out to our house to help. Arnold Torres from Daystar had also recommended Don to us. We knew Don, and this was confirmation that he was the one to use. Through the years, I have told Steve, "God knew when He gave you the name Wisdom that you would be very wise."

When I went shopping for a new car, I looked at different car dealers. I had to decide which car would be right for me. Angela and I went to several different dealers. I thought about how Claude would go about making a decision on buying a car and what things he would require.

I wanted comfort in the front and back seats, a warranty, the right color, the right size, a sunroof, and Bluetooth, and the price had to fit my budget. How the dealership dealt with me made a big difference too, because many businesses take advantage of women (especially widows).

Freeman Toyota was my choice, because it had a car that fit all my requirements. I enjoyed working with their courteous staff: Steve Curry, David McClanahan, Trent Boe, and James Robert Morris, who is the son of Pastor Robert Morris at Gateway Church. They are a blessing to me and have become my friends.

Everyone I met who worked there is a Christian, and we would talk about Jesus. They saw me at my worst due to the stress of losing my husband and buying a car without him to help make the final decision.

I can say not one person got upset with me. I always have a nice visit when I go there. Trent gave me three free oil changes and also told me to bring my car in if it needed washing; it would be free.

Steve, David, and James make sure that my car gets washed when I go into the dealership. I had a great experience buying my new car. Buy yourself a new car if you can so you will feel secure when you have to travel.

If you don't have an alarm system in your house, I suggest you get one. We had an alarm system that covered the doors only. I called the company and had the system installed on the windows too. It just gives you that added sense of security and lets you rest much better at night knowing you are completely protected.

If your spouse retires, my advice is to take the opportunity to stay home together by retiring too. I had only four years to be with Claude after I retired.

Although I loved working at Daystar, I felt compelled to retire and stay at home with him. When I would come home from work, I could always tell how lonely he had been while I was away. It was hard to leave Daystar, but I knew I was supposed to. I now know why I felt that way.

God knew it was nearing Claude's time to go to heaven. He ordered my steps, and I am so glad he did send me home to be with my husband. We did whatever we wanted to, and only God was our Boss. We didn't have to punch a time clock and we could stay up late if we wanted to. We were bosom buddies, and we enjoyed each other's company so much.

I made some adjustments in my house to make it more economical for me after Claude's passing.

I have a big upstairs, so Claude Jr. and I came up with these ideas. Claude and I had already put a damper upstairs for the heater and air conditioner, so we could control the temperature up there.

I don't use the upstairs that much, so we decided to have a curtain made to curve around the bottom of the stairway that makes a barrier to keep the heat downstairs in the wintertime and the cool downstairs in the summertime. This way, I would heat or cool only the floor that I was using.

I called a professional out to give me an estimate, and I chose Bobales Driskill's Interiors. She did a superb job. I have seen a reduction in my electric and gas bills since doing that.

My son came up with the idea to install a change-over switch that hooks to the breaker panel. We would have it put close to the generator on my screened-in porch. That way, I wouldn't have cords all over the floor of my house when I needed to use the generator. I only have to pull the switch and—voila!—electricity!

Howard Meister, my friend (and now husband) offered to come out and do this work for me, as I shared in chapter fourteen. What a generous thing for him to do! He taught me how to use the transfer switch, and when he turned off the electricity to test it the generator gave me electricity where Howard had arranged for it to go. It was so neat to see all of his hard work produce the end results.

I am so grateful to him for doing that for me. I do not ever want to take for granted anything anyone does for me. That is why I have shared about those who have done things for me.

Howard has helped me in many other ways: he's fixed my swing, my lawnmower belt, showerhead, attic door, front glass door, and water fountain and cut off the edge of a table that I kept running into and cutting my arm. He adjusted the roof turbines and showed me how to work and use many things.

He is a top-notch *Howard-of-all-trades*. What a blessing he has been to me—an angel in disguise. I call him a *Meister crafter,* and he certainly is one.

Angela found and bought some coin collector pages for her dad's coins at Hobby Lobby. I filled them with coins, but soon found I would have to go back to the store and buy more pages.

I also bought an album to keep the pages in. It took me about a month to go through all the coins and put them in the album. I arranged them in order by the year they were minted. Some of them were very old. I did this to honor my husband and his hobby.

When I completed that task, I began to write this book. Everything I have set my hand to do has been healing therapy for me.

I would encourage you to finish things that your loved one didn't get to finish. It will bring you so much joy to lift it up to heaven and say, as I did, "I have finished your hobby for you, honey. I know this is as important to you as it has been for me doing it for you."

I know Claude was pleased that I completed his coin collection, and it blessed me to do it for him.

Exercise is important for your health, and it helps to relieve stress. I joined Curves to exercise and keep me feeling well. Jeanine Novotny and Sharon Kenna, the owners, are very nice. Brenda Read and Nancy Carlson are wonderful trainers. They all were a blessing to me.

I enjoyed exercising with my friends Linda Boyd, Sue Hatmaker, and Diane Runnells. All of these people have helped on me my journey of healing. Sue Hatmaker joined about the same time as I did.

Sue came to the hospital the night Claude went to heaven. Sue took me out to eat at a nice tearoom and the food was delicious. It is nice to have friends who are an encouragement.

Claude and I used to walk at the mall for exercise. I still go there occasionally, but I go to Curves more now. My insurance pays for it, so I wanted to take advantage of it. I encourage you to get into some kind of exercise program to help you become physically fit and relieve any stress you may have. We all have stress from time to time.

Treat yourself to whatever you like to eat and go out with your friends. Make it a priority to enjoy yourself so you can have fun. I enjoy getting an all-natural fruit smoothie at the Smoothie King. Yummy!

My sister, Charlotte, and her husband, Gary, took me to the movies and out to eat. I spent the night with them and really enjoyed myself. I had not been to a 3-D movie since I was a teenager. It was fun looking through glasses to watch a movie. It was a change of pace for me and took my mind off missing Claude. Thanks to Charlotte and Gary, it lifted my spirit.

Gary fried us some fish the next day and made a great salad, and it sure was good.

I played with their dogs; they are so sweet, another step on the road to regaining joy in my life. Two of the dogs, Happy and Casey, used to be our dogs.

After Claude and I retired, we gave them to Gary and Charlotte. They have treated the dogs like royalty. They really love and enjoy them. They are great "dog parents."

My brother, Oscar Dale, took me to the fiftieth wedding anniversary party for my cousins Brenda and Tom, and then we went out to eat.

My parents, sisters and brother and I and we make a marvelous family.

My parents had seven girls and one boy: Oscar Dale. He has been a blessing to me. He survived living with seven sisters—yeah! So if someone wants to take you somewhere, go with them and start enjoying life again.

Jim, Claudanna Wedding with many family members.

Yorks and Eckharts with our children in El Paso, Texas

Mother, her son and six daughters on Eckhart's staircase we are so neat.

Curington - Miller cousins are so cute and not all cousins got to be there.

When we had our back porch screened in, Oscar Dale brought us a hammock for it. We have really enjoyed that hammock. He calls to check on me a lot since I have been alone.

He told me Claude was like a big brother and he was going to miss him.

One day, Oscar Dale came to my house with a huge box of apples. I decided to make apple cobblers for him and each of my children. I had not been cooking very much, but I did it, and they were very good—if I do say so myself. Thanks, Oscar Dale.

Kathy, a friend of mine, took me to a movie and I really enjoyed our time together. It helped to take my mind off missing Claude. Kathy had become a widow before I did, so she knew what I was experiencing. Kathy has been there to help me any way she could since Claude was promoted to heaven.

We go to the same church and sometimes go out to eat together. We also go to the same home group, a small group of Christians who meet to study the Bible and share our blessings. Kathy has sent me cards and called me many times just to check on me. She has been a good friend who lives by the Word.

Margaret became my friend when I worked at Daystar. She also has taken me out to eat, and we had good food and sweet fellowship. After we finished our meal, she took me to see her new house. It was so lovely. I am so happy for her, because she really deserves it.

It lifts your spirits to go out with your friends and family. Make this a priority, because it is a real mood lifter.

I took my book over to show Patty, my neighbor. I had just planned to show her the cover, but she insisted that I leave it with her so she could read what I had written so far. Patty told me that she had tutored students who were deaf when she worked at a nearby college. She said she would be glad to show me anything that I should change.

I had prayed that very day for God to give me the next step for my book. I knew I would have to find someone to proofread my book before I took it to a publisher. I was so glad Patty offered to help me with that. Patty is a wonderful neighbor and friend. I thank God for Patty and Vernon. Thanks to sweet Patty for using her talent to improve my book.

One day I said, "God I have never written a book before or even thought about writing a book. God, I know you put that desire in my heart, not just for me but for those who are alone like I have been. I know how you helped me to be an overcomer and become an eagle."

I sing this very old hymn a lot—"Never Alone"—because I am alone so much. Sometimes, it gets so lonely that I just begin to sing this hymn. Here is a part of what I sing.

I've heard the voice of my Savior, telling me still to fight on. I feel a peace in knowing, my Savior stands between. He stands to shield me from danger, when earthly friends are gone. He promised never to leave me, never to leave me alone. "No never alone!" "No never alone!" Jesus promised never to leave me, never to leave me alone.

I was four years old when this hymn was written.

My parents, Oscar and Dorothy Curington, took our family to the Baptist church and they would always sing this song. As a young girl, I loved to sing it. It still releases joy in my soul and gives me peace.

I had not sung this hymn in many years until I was alone without my sweet Claude. You can never lose your memories, even from your childhood. If you have a song that can uplift your spirit, just sing, sing. No one can hear you except Jesus.

I believe restoration in your life and mine is not about covering up the hurt and grief; it's about getting totally healed.

I want to continue my journey in my life, going forward and not going backward. Life isn't about waiting for the storm to pass. It is dancing with the wind, learning to dance in the storm and dancing like no one is watching.

Chapter Eighteen

MAKE SURE YOU ARE READY

I WANT TO ENCOURAGE YOU TO REMEMBER to take one day at a time and discover your purpose and the destiny God has planned for you. That is what I am doing.

My assignment has not been completed. I am on that journey though, for it to be fulfilled. When I leave this world and I am out of here, hey, guess what? I will have finished my assignment. Don't worry, folks, this is God's plan for you and for me. I intend to follow His plan. Do you know what your assignment is on this earth?

Projects are vital to our mental health. There is no limit to realizing our potential. In our later years, we have more time to expand our horizons, because we are free from our former routines. We may be retired, but we should desire to fulfill our potential in life. I want to be yearning and not yawning.

I want to go forward in my life to do whatever God has planned for me. I want a fresh run at life. I want to be an overcomer and to broaden my interests in new ways to the glory of God.

If you take time to look forward and inward, you may be surprised at your own creativity, ingenuity, and originality.

You will be surprised to find that you can do things you have never done before. We need to believe in ourselves and know that we are capable and can do some new things, even when we no longer have our spouses. The same thing applies, when we still have our spouses too.

I believe we can experience a rebirth of creativity with newfound gifts. I also believe that God is the provider of all good gifts and He will rekindle within us buried talents that we neglected in our earlier years.

Because I married so young, I think I didn't give myself that opportunity. When I was young, I never asked God what my purpose in life was; I guess I didn't know I was supposed to. I just wanted to get away from home and get married.

I am now at a place in my life that I am asking God, "What do you want me to do?"

I am excited about the new things God has planned for me! I will not leave this earth until I have fulfilled His purpose. I am focusing on hearing from God and discovering the destiny that I know only He can make happen. I know only God can do it because He had already made the plans for my life before I was even formed in my mother's womb.

God has a Plan A for me, and there is no Plan B. I need to go with the flow and wait to hear from God. This is where my future lies.

Early in his life, Claude accepted Jesus as his Savior. If he had not yet done that, there would have been no time, because he passed so quickly. He was sleeping, then just drew his last breath peacefully and went to heaven with no pain. I wish he had at least been able to hear me tell him I loved him. It happened so fast that I was unable to talk with him or tell him good-bye.

When people have finished their assignment with joy on earth and they go home to be with Jesus, nothing can change that. I did pray for Claude to come back, but he didn't. So I knew he had accomplished his work here on earth.

I beg you to be ready for when your assignment on earth is done. It is a simple prayer of asking Jesus to come in your heart, asking him to forgive you of all your sins, and making Him Number One in your life. This commitment you make to him will allow heaven to welcome you there too.

We can have no idols in our lives. An idol is anything we put first in our lives before Jesus. There is a heaven to gain and a hell to shun.

That is why I told Jesus in the emergency room, "I love Claude with all my heart, but Jesus, I love you more." Jesus has to be our first love and our Lord and Savior in our lives.

I want my book to encourage every reader to seek God our Maker, the Author and Finisher of our life.

Danva's Budget

DECIDE ON THE
AMOUNT YOU NEED.

WHEN YOU PRAY, ASK IN FAITH and believe that you receive it (Matthew 21:22).

When you ask God, be very specific about what you are going to believe Him for.

Believe without doubt (Mark 11:22–24 and James 1:6).

Always pay your tithe off the gross amount.

When extra money comes in, do not spend it all.

Begin to apply extra money to your smallest bill.

When that bill is paid off, apply that extra money to your next larger bill.

Continue to do this until you eliminate all of the bills.

Believe to be debt-free (Romans 13:8).

Be "seed-minded" and not "need-minded."

Template starts on the next page.

TEMPLATE

SAMPLE BUDGET

THIS IS THE DEBT-FREE BUDGET YOU are going to believe God for. Using the bills you owe now, make a budget following this sample budget guideline. Make a goal for your budget to be like the sample budget, and this is a faith step.

1. Tithe (off the Gross Amount)	$
2. Pay Yourself (Savings)	$
3. Pledges	$
4. Offerings	$
5. Help Others	$
6. Groceries	$
7. House Payment	Paid Off
8. Car Payments	Paid Off
9. Car Insurance	$
10. Burial Policy	Paid Off
11. Life Insurance	$
12. Health Insurance	$
13. Credit Cards	Paid Off
14. Electric Bill	$
15. Gas Bill	$
16. Water Bill	$
17. Phone Bill	$
18. Gasoline for Car	$
19. Meals Out	$

20. Clothes	$
21. Presents (Birthdays, etc.)	$
22. Miscellaneous	$
23. Spending Money	$
Total (Weekly or Monthly)	$

Terri Copeland Pearsons: Words of Encouragement, Prophecy, and Her Prayer

12-02-09

My dad, Kenneth Copeland, explained the following to a man the other day and you can claim it for yourself:

Claude is in Christ. Danva, you are in Jesus. Christ is in you Danva. Jesus is in Claude.

So you are in one another.

You are going to have to develop, through Jesus, a new relationship with Claude. You have a relationship with Jesus. You will talk with Claude, just like when you talk to Jesus.

Resist loss. It will take you down a dark path. Do not give the Devil a chance to do anything.

Roll your cares on the Lord and just trust God. Believe Jesus bore your grief.

Pastor Terri Copeland Pearsons Prophecy:

"Danva there is going to be an unusual amount of grace upon you. It will turn your eyes to God for His will, purpose, and His plan for you. As you draw closer and closer to Him, there will be strength and He will satisfy every longing of your heart."

Pastor Terri Copeland Pearsons Prayer:

Jesus, you are very worthy to be thanked, for giving Danva grace, peace, wisdom, and provision. "Thank you Jesus," for increasing grace to Danva as she steps into your peace. Amen!

CLAUDE'S LOVE NOTES

I WAS ALWAYS FINDING LOVE NOTES FROM Claude in my Bibles, by my bed, chairs, wherever he decided to put them. He even wrote notes on my mirrors, telling me that he loved me.

The other day, I was reading out of one of Claude's Bibles. It was in his Living Bible at Psalm 103:5 and it touched me very much. Right by the Scripture that says, "God fills my life with good things," Claude had written, "God gave me Danva to love." Claude wrote again at the top of the page in the Bible, he wrote Psalm 103:5 and *God gave me Danva to love.*

He was a good husband and I truly knew that I was loved by Claude.

I miss Claude so very much, our marriage, his faith in God, his love, his wisdom, his companionship, his friendship, his integrity, his faithfulness, his sense of humor, and most of all, him.

God blessed me with Claude and I do appreciate all the time that I had with him. Two weeks before Claude went to heaven, he typed me a love note. I was on the computer when Claude walked into the room. I asked him if he would like to type something on the computer, and he said, "Yes."

He used to get on the computer at his work, but he did not want to at home. I did not know then why I even asked him if he wanted to type something. I know now that God was letting him type his last love note to me. God knew his assignment was soon to be over and in two weeks he would be in heaven.

This is my love note from Claude, just the way he typed it.

CLAUDE RAY YORK SR.
I LOVE DANVA YORK WITH ALL MY HEART FOREVER
YOU ARE BEAUTIFUL ALL OVER BABYDOLL
LOVE CLAUDE RAY

What an honor to be loved so much by Claude for forty-four years!

I do long for the day Claude will meet me at the gate of heaven. I know he is in my future.

Claude served Jesus as a soldier and he has gained his wings like a soldier for our country.

I know Claude sings in the choir of heaven and he is waiting for me to sing with him too!

A picture of Claude now he is in heaven in his mansion wearing white too.

Meditations on Scriptures for Widows

GOD IS MY HUSBAND

I PARAPHRASED THESE SCRIPTURES AND WROTE THEM personally for myself. I confessed them daily out loud. Doing this was a great comfort to me and a vital part of my life.

Isaiah 54:5 – For my Maker is my husband; the Lord of Hosts is His name.

Job 29:13 – God will cause my widow's heart to sing for joy.

Psalm 68:5 – God is the protector of me, the widow, who is God in His holy habitation.

Psalm 146:9 – The Lord upholds me, the widow, sets me upright, and will provide for me.

Proverbs 15:25 – The Lord will make secure the boundaries of me, the consecrated widow.

Isaiah 54:4 – I will not fear, for I shall not be ashamed. Nor will I be confounded, confused, or depressed, for I shall not be put to shame, for I shall not (seriously) remember the reproach of my widowhood anymore.

Jeremiah 49:11 – I am a widow, but I will trust and confide in God.

Matthew 6:25 – I will not worry about my life, what I shall eat or drink, my body, or what I should wear. Is not my life more important than food and my body more important than clothes? I can look at the birds of the air; they do not sow or reap or store away in barns, and yet my heavenly Father feeds them. I will trust You, God, to do the same thing for me! (NIV).

1Timothy 5:5 – I will fix my hope as a widow on You, God, and I will pray.

Deuteronomy 10:17 – God, You will execute justice for me, the widow, and give me food and clothing.

2 Corinthians 1:2–4 – Grace, favor, and spiritual blessing to me and (heart) peace from God my Father and my Lord Jesus Christ, the Messiah, the Anointed One. Blessed be my God and Father of my Lord Jesus Christ, the Father of sympathy (pity and mercy) and the *God (who is the Source) of my every consolation and comfort and encouragement;* Jesus consoles, comforts, and encourages me in everything, so that I may also be able to console (comfort and encourage) those who are in any kind of trouble or distress, with the consolation (comfort and encouragement) with which I am consoled, comforted, and encouraged by my God.

Danva's Song: My Widow's Tears

God, you wiped away all my tears.
God, you wiped away all my fears.
All the grief and sorrow cannot stay.
Because, God, you removed them all today.
You have taken all the grief and sadness.
You have restored all my joy and gladness.
I will praise you, and I will worship your holy name.
My life I give to you; it will never be the same.
It will release a new chapter and beginnings in my life
That you planned for me even before I was a wife.
Danva York
02–02–10

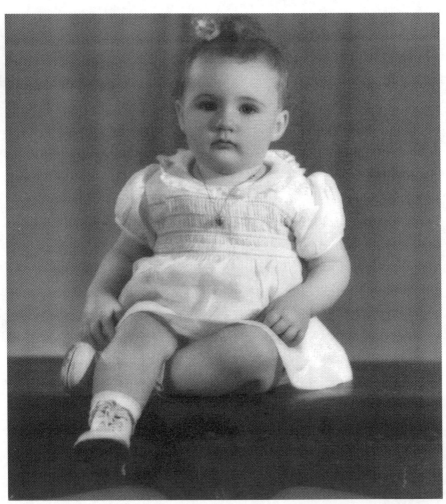

I am sitting on a table as a baby and God had already planned my life.

*I am now leaning on a table as a woman. God's plan
for me to write this book has been revealed. It took years
for this to unfold now the story can be told.*

Howard and Danva, we stand with gratefulness that God joined us together.

Howard and Danva, we have a knowing look of love, our destiny together.

Expressions of Awe

I AM FILLED WITH AWE TO HAVE written this book and to know that God's handwriting was on the walls of my life. Writing this book has proven to me I don't have to plan my life, because God already has.

I am awestruck to see how He chose each season of my life and He chose who I would share my journey with. My husbands, children, grandchildren, other relatives, and friends have touched me in a way that only God could have planned.

I want to encourage everyone to get excited about life. Sing even if you can't carry a tune. Love like no one has ever hurt you, and don't forget to dance too.

Life is made up of the ingredients that God used to design us. God did not make a mistake when he created us. *Awww,* He really designed us for a purpose.

We all go through seasons in our lives, and as difficult as some might be, we can't quit too soon. Otherwise, we will never experience the rewards that are waiting for us at the end.

The best is yet to come. I am a living example of this, and it all adds up to amazing awe.

God's plan for us is to be completely satisfied with awe of His remarkable destiny He has for us. He excites me with the awe of His love that He gives to each of us too.

A majestic, splendid, restored confidence of awe has been imparted into me. I can go on in this life excited to see what is ahead for me. I hope you can get excited about your future too.

Swing across time in awe, and let life bless you. I hope I have encouraged you.

The best expression of awe to me is that my God is an awesome, good God!

Jesus loves you, and I do too.

Danva York Meister